Active Shooter

Events and Response

Active Shooter
Events and Response

J. Pete Blair • Terry Nichols
David Burns • John R. Curnutt

CRC Press
Taylor & Francis Group
Boca Raton   London   New York

CRC Press is an imprint of the
Taylor & Francis Group, an **informa** business

Cover photo: Diana Hendricks

CRC Press
Taylor & Francis Group
6000 Broken Sound Parkway NW, Suite 300
Boca Raton, FL 33487-2742

© 2013 by Taylor & Francis Group, LLC
CRC Press is an imprint of Taylor & Francis Group, an Informa business

No claim to original U.S. Government works

Printed on acid-free paper
Version Date: 20130514

International Standard Book Number-13: 978-1-4665-1229-0 (Hardback)

Library of Congress Cataloging-in-Publication Data

Blair, John P., 1971-
    Active shooter events and response / John P. Blair, Terry Nichols, David Burns, and John R. Curnutt.
        pages cm
    Includes bibliographical references and index.
    ISBN 978-1-4665-1229-0 (alk. paper)
    1. Mass murder--United States. 2. Law enforcement--United States--Planning. 3. Emergency management--United States. I. Title.

HV6529.B534 2013
363.2'3--dc23   2013004179

Visit the Taylor & Francis Web site at
http://www.taylorandfrancis.com

and the CRC Press Web site at
http://www.crcpress.com

Contents

Preface

Prior to the tragic events at Columbine High School on April 20, 1999, the term "active shooter" was not a household word or a news headline flashing across the screens of our televisions. Although there had been numerous mass shootings across the United States prior to this tragedy, this one event not only single-handedly changed our country's view on school safety, but also significantly changed the law enforcement response to mass shootings. Outdated police response strategies were replaced with new, aggressive tactics to be used by the first officers on the scene of a mass shooting. National training programs and standards were implemented to ensure that all first responding law enforcement personnel were properly and consistently trained to address the active shooter threat. Unfortunately, mass shootings continue to occur, making national headlines almost monthly.

During the final days of completing the manuscript for this book, another unthinkable mass shooting tragedy occurred, this time at Sandy Hook Elementary School in Newtown, Connecticut. On Friday, December 14, 2012, a suspect forced his way into the locked elementary school where he systematically shot and killed 20 children, aged 6 to 7 years, along with 6 female teachers and staff. A swift response by local and state law enforcement prevented the situation from being much worse; however, this recent event should again remind us all about the importance of training and preparing for these critical situations before they occur in our own backyards.

The law enforcement profession must continue to examine each and every active shooter or mass killing event and learn from them to prepare for the future. This book is one of the first known attempts not only to discuss historical active shooter events, but also actually dissect some of the critical, high-profile events to gain the knowledge and experience from those who have gone before us. It also offers insight into training methodologies and strategies used for preparing our nation's first responders to address the active shooter threat. In addition, the clear and present threat of terrorist organizations using this tactic on American soil, similar to the attacks in Beslan, Russia and Mumbai, India, is discussed, along with the training implications for our civilian law enforcement personnel.

This book is written by members of the Advanced Law Enforcement Rapid Response Training (ALERRT) Center at Texas State University. Since its founding in 2002, ALERRT has trained more than 40,000 law enforcement officers from 41 states and the District of Columbia in active shooter response. ALERRT has also trained first responders in Brazil and Canada as well as officers from the United Kingdom, Finland, and Portugal. Additionally, ALERRT has an active research program that examines not only active shooter events, but also best practices in response to these events. The information presented here is the culmination of more than a decade's worth of training and research into active shooter events and represents what we believe to be state-of-the-art, evidence-based best practices.

As you read this book, take note that we never use the suspects' names when discussing specific events. Many active shooters appear to be motivated by a desire for fame (or perhaps, more appropriately, infamy). We choose not to help these cowards obtain their desire for recognition. Instead, we refer to them only as suspect, attacker, or shooter. It is, in our opinion, tragic that their names are used as often as they are and that some have become household names. Our focus is and will always be on the victims and first responders. This book is dedicated to those innocent victims whose lives have been cut tragically short and those first responders who are willing to put their lives at risk for others and be that "thin blue line."

Acknowledgments

There are many individuals who should be recognized for their invaluable assistance with our understanding of and knowledge about the active shooter threat. Although we fear that we will undoubtedly fail to recognize some who have been critically important to each of us over the past 10 years, rest assured that we owe you all a great deal of gratitude and a sincere "thank-you!"

The ALERRT Center at Texas State University-San Marcos was the dream of a few and the result of the efforts of many. Forward-thinking police administrators, including Chief Steve Griffith and Sheriff Don Montague, recognized the need for this invaluable training and empowered us to chase a dream and a vision. Professionals from the academic arena, including Dr. Bill Covington, Dr. Carolyn Pate, Dr. Quint Thurman, and Dr. Tom Mijares, heard the passionate pleas from those of us seeking a way to provide critical training to frontline officers and were instrumental in securing funding to create ALERRT.

The Texas Tactical Police Officers Association (TTPOA) also played an integral role in the development of standardized active shooter training. They were one of the first organizations to recognize the monumental shift in traditional tactical thinking after the Columbine tragedy and immediately began pushing training out to first responders. We owe a debt of gratitude to Officer Marcus "Sandy" Wall, Lieutenant John "Doc" Dombrowa, and Sergeant Stuart Red for introducing us to a training methodology and curriculum that became the foundation of the ALERRT program.

Diana Hendricks has been the director of communications for the ALERRT program since its inception. She took on and accepted the mission of adding visual enhancements to our training manuals, producing promotional materials, articulating beautifully the need for training, and crunching numbers on grant applications. Diana continues to coordinate every class delivered by the ALERRT program (as well as many other things) and we can attest that we would not be where we are today without her energy, efforts, and incredible talent.

We have all been blessed over the years to have trained with some of the best tactical operators and gifted instructors from law enforcement and the military. Each of these individuals has left lasting impressions on us all. MSG Paul Howe, US Army, retired, has been instrumental in our development as operators, instructors, leaders, and humans. We are all honored to have worked with Paul over the years and are privileged to call him a friend. Tracy Weems was also instrumental in the development of our civilian response model.

We are proud not only to call Mark Cumberland, Jeff Waters, Armando Ramirez, and dozens of professional warrior trainers adjunct instructors but also brothers and sisters. Their dedication and pursuit of excellence has, in our opinion, formed the greatest assembly of tactical instructors in the world.

We would also like to thank M. Hunter Martaindale, doctoral student in the School of Criminal Justice at Texas State University, for his work in preparing the appendix and his contributions to Chapter 3.

Last but not least—and actually most importantly, we would like to thank our families. Anna, Tiffany, Nicky, and all of our respective children have been patient over the years as we followed what can only be considered a "calling."

Authors

J. Pete Blair is an associate professor of criminal justice at Texas State University and the director of research for ALERRT. Dr. Blair earned his PhD in criminal justice from Michigan State University and his bachelor's and master's degrees in law enforcement and justice administration from Western Illinois University. His current research deals with active shooter events and best practices. He has published research on a variety of policing issues in numerous journal articles and book chapters.

David Burns has been a deputy sheriff in Texas since 1995 and is one of the founding members of the ALERRT program. He also currently serves as a SWAT team leader, where he has been assigned since 1997. Prior to law enforcement, David served for 7 years with the US Army's 82nd Airborne Division and is a veteran of the Persian Gulf War.

Terry Nichols is the assistant director of the ALERRT Center at Texas State University-San Marcos. Terry retired from the San Marcos Police Department at the rank of commander in January 2010 after serving over 21 years with the department. His last assignment included commanding the Criminal Investigation Division as well as the Hays County SWAT team, where he served for over 10 years. Terry worked numerous assignments for the department over his career, including patrol, narcotics, training, and administration. During his tenure in the Training Division, Terry led the development and creation of the ALERRT Center in San Marcos. He has a BS degree (1991) and an MS degree (1997) from Southwest Texas State University.

John Curnutt has been a police officer in Texas since 1995 and is the director of training for ALERRT. John has been with the training program since the beginning. He is also a SWAT team leader with over 14 years of experience on the team. John's past assignments with his agency include working as a School Resource Officer (SRO) in the patrol division. Prior to law enforcement, he studied criminal justice at Texas State University-San Marcos after serving in the US Army's Arctic Light Infantry immediately after high school.

Chapter 1

Historical Perspective of Active Shooter Events

Introduction

There are numerous instances, throughout history, where deranged suspects have sought out and killed as many innocent victims as possible. These mass murderers, also referred to as "active shooters" since the Columbine High School tragedy in April 1999, have presented a unique tactical challenge to law enforcement officers. In many ways, law enforcement tactics in addressing these active shooters have come full circle in the past 46 years.

During the early morning hours of August 1, 1966, a former United States Marine and current student at the University of Texas murdered his mother as she slept in her Austin, Texas home. The suspect then returned to his home where he killed his wife of 4 years as she slept. After typing and handwriting suicide notes, the suspect took a cache of weapons in a footlocker to the University of Texas Tower and made his way up to the 27th floor. When asked for his university identification by the observation deck receptionist, the suspect beat her with a rifle and hid her body behind furniture. The receptionist,

Edna Townsley, later died from her injuries and became the third victim to be killed that day.

As the suspect made his way up the final flight of stairs to the observation deck, he barricaded the stairway to create a stronghold. Before the suspect made it outside to the observation deck, two families came up on the barricaded stairway and encountered him in the stairwell. He fired on the families, killing two people and seriously wounding two more. Once the shooter was established on the observation deck with his footlocker full of weapons, a new tactical dilemma faced the Austin Police Department: how to stop a barricaded, military trained sniper, who held a 28-story elevated position over the University of Texas campus, from killing victims at will?

Unfortunately for the Austin Police Department, special weapons and tactics (SWAT) teams did not exist in 1966. It was not that the city of Austin, Texas was a small, rural police agency and simply did not have the resources to field a SWAT team; rather, these types of units and the acronym SWAT simply did not exist at that time. Tactical situations, like the University of Texas sniper, had to be resolved by patrol officers who had little, if any, tactical training and even less equipment available to them. Hostage situations, barricaded gunmen, and high-risk warrants were all handled by the patrol officer on the street. Critical, violent events like the UT Tower shooting and the Watts riots in 1965 led to the creation of specialized tactical units across the nation.

With no specialized tactical units they could call to help resolve the barricaded sniper on the UT Tower, Austin police officers Houston McCoy, Ramiro Martinez, and Jerry Day, along with citizen Allen Crum, made their way up the tower to stop the suspect's rampage. Stopping along the way to quickly help the wounded and develop an ad hoc plan to assault the observation deck, the officers ultimately pushed past the barricades and stepped onto the observation deck where the suspect continued to fire on innocent civilians below. Once on the deck, the officers then had to stay low and carefully avoid the shots from police officers and civilians below who were all shooting at the suspect.

The officers split up and traced the sounds of gunfire coming from the suspect's rifle to the northwest corner of the observation deck. Once they had identified the suspect sitting down and firing a rifle toward the crowds below, Officer Martinez fired his service revolver six times and Officer McCoy fired his duty shotgun twice, striking and killing the suspect. These patrol officers, neither of whom had any tactical training or specialized equipment, had successfully stopped the worst mass shooting in the United States up until that time.

Specialization of the Police

The 1960s and 1970s brought unique challenges and changes to American law enforcement. First, cultural and social issues required the police to become increasingly engaged in managing demonstrations, many of which became violent. The war in Vietnam, coupled with the ongoing civil rights movement, led to numerous large-scale skirmishes between citizens and the police. Events such as the August 28, 1968, riots in Chicago during the Democratic National Convention; the August 1965 Watts riots in Los Angeles; and the shooting deaths of four college students by Ohio National Guard troops at Kent State University led to increased tensions and open hostility between citizens and the government.

Second, research on the police and policing function began in earnest, much of it funded by the Law Enforcement Assistance Administration (LEAA) and later by the National Institute of Justice (NIJ). In 1965, President Lyndon Johnson appointed the President's Crime Commission, which endorsed an agenda of professionalization, higher recruitment standards, more training, and better management and supervision in the 1967 report titled *The Challenge of Crime in a Free Society* (Walker and Katz 2005). Research projects such as the Kansas

City Preventive Patrol Experiment (1972–1973) challenged long-held assumptions about the role of patrol officers in preventing and suppressing crime.

Third, advances in technology began making their way into policing at all levels. From more efficient radio communications to advanced weapons and tactical equipment, technological developments changed the way patrol officers performed their jobs (Mijares, McCarthy, and Perkins 2000). The introduction of office computers led to the creation of computer aided dispatching (CAD), more efficient record keeping, and database management, as well as the initiation of the Automated Fingerprint Identification System (AFIS).

The push for increased education, training, and professionalism for the police, coupled with the rapid integration of new equipment and technologies into the policing profession, began a new era of specialization in police functions. Whereas prior to this time, patrol officers, outside major agencies in large cities, were responsible for basically all policing functions, the 1970s and 1980s saw a dramatic swing away from this "generalist" functionality of the patrol officer. Specialized units and functions, including SWAT teams, crime scene technicians, gang units, narcotics units, traffic specialists, motor units, photography, domestic violence units, and repeat offender units, were created in even the smallest of jurisdictions. Of all the specialization areas, the creation of tactical units, or SWAT teams, became one of the most visible and hotly debated specializations and that debate continues today.

The need for civilian law enforcement to have the capability to respond to critical, violent events is without debate. Events such as the University of Texas Tower shooting, the Watts riots, and a 24-hour sniper standoff at a Howard Johnson's Motel in New Orleans in 1972, to name a few, ultimately led to the creation of specialized tactical units (Mijares et al. 2000). Police administrators quickly learned that the nature and complexity of tactical situations were changing. Criminals were becoming better armed through the availability of large-capacity firearms after the Vietnam War. Offenders often had negative and hostile views toward law enforcement and the government in general, leading to violent stand-offs. Containing violent situations became a major challenge for even the largest of agencies. Agencies ultimately needed specialists who were trained to plan and respond to critical incidents as a coordinated unit without depleting the agency's personnel or ability to handle routine calls for service (Mijares et al. 2000).

Tactical teams were created and established to address specific threat situations that had historically challenged responding officers, law enforcement agencies, and the communities they served. Responding to situations such as barricaded suspects, hostage situations, high-risk warrants, and snipers became the responsibility of these specialized tactical units. Large metropolitan agencies such as the Los Angeles Police Department, New York Police Department, Houston Police Department, and others created full-time tactical units who had no other job responsibility than to train and respond to critical incidents. Smaller agencies that did not have the personnel to staff a full-time tactical unit created part-time SWAT teams. These officers were typically assigned patrol or investigation functions, with SWAT being a collateral duty to their primary job. Many areas combined their part-time teams and formed multiagency, regional SWAT teams to share assets and resources.

The emergence and explosion of tactical teams across the country was fueled not only by necessity, but also by the perceived glamour and awe of the SWAT officer. First, in 1975, the television series *S.W.A.T.* debuted, giving television viewers a glimpse of what Hollywood believed tactical officers did every day on the job. As described by the International Movie Database (IMDb), the plot summary "features the missions of the Los Angeles Police Department's Special Weapons and Tactics Team. They are a team of highly trained and heavily armed police officers whose purpose is to make coordinated assaults on armed and dangerous criminals in sensitive situations and defensible locations." Secondly, young police officers are typically not drawn into law enforcement to handle barking dog complaints, take theft reports, and take on welfare concerns. Although making their communities a safer place and serving the public are common ideals, most officers desire some action and want to be on the frontlines chasing down suspects and catching the bad guys. When a SWAT team was seen rolling out to a scene and conducting a tactical operation, almost every young officer wanted to be that "knight in black Velcro"—the specialist who came to save the day.

Additionally, the SWAT teams received all of the latest tools and equipment to use for tactical operations. Weapons and equipment such as automatic weapons, rifles, heavy body armor, flashbangs, tactical shields, helmets, and tear gas were standard equipment for SWAT teams. For many agencies, surplus military equipment, including armored vehicles and night-vision equipment, was a cost-effective means for outfitting their SWAT teams. Officers assigned to tactical teams, whether full-time or part-time teams, often had take-home cars and personalized equipment that patrol officers were lacking.

Finally, officers assigned to SWAT teams received far more training than their counterparts assigned to different nontactical functions. The nature of the tactical assignment required a significant investment in training SWAT officers. Tactical officers had to be proficient in many different disciplines within the tactical arena, including advanced shooting, breaching, assault techniques, rappelling, chemical agents, flashbang deployment, and night vision. In addition to individual skills, members of tactical teams had to train as a team. In high-risk operations and environments, teamwork and trust are critical components for successful outcomes. In the end, SWAT teams were successful because they had advanced equipment, were properly trained with that equipment, and worked together as a cohesive team to accomplish their missions.

Over time, specialized units slowly eroded the responsibilities of patrol officers. Once crime scene units were established, patrol officers who had traditionally taken crime scene photographs and dusted for latent fingerprints now simply took the initial information from a complainant or victim and called for the crime scene specialist to respond. If faced with a juvenile suspect, patrol officers could turn the suspect over to an investigator who would conduct the investigation. In cases of domestic violence, many agencies created specialists who would respond to the scene of any domestic violence call to take over the investigation.

When patrol officers and supervisors found themselves faced with a serious tactical situation—such as an armed and barricaded suspect, hostage situation, or high-risk warrant that needed to be served—they called the SWAT team. In the event of an in-progress crime, such as a hostage situation or armed, barricaded suspect where patrol officers were the first on the scene, the patrol role became that of containment. Although they had little if any formal training on how to contain these types of tactical situations, patrol officers were tasked to wait for the SWAT teams to arrive and take over. This response strategy, often referred to as the "Four Cs" (contain, control, communicate, call SWAT), became a standard patrol officer response protocol. In cases where patrol officers did take initiative and resolved or attempted to resolve a situation prior to SWAT arrival, they were often chastised and administratively punished for stepping outside their role and training.

Patrol officers received very little advanced tactical and decision-making training prior to 1999. This preparedness gap led to situations where patrol officers would try to resolve a tactical situation better suited for a SWAT team and ultimately make it worse, sometimes leading to the deaths of the patrol officers themselves.

For example, on a December night in 1999 in Hays County, Texas, a patrol officer initiated a vehicle pursuit that eventually terminated once the suspect lost control of the vehicle and crashed. The suspect exited the vehicle with a handgun held up to his head creating a standoff with the pursuing officers. Prior to the officers containing the suspect and creating a suitable perimeter, the suspect walked freely around a neighborhood taunting officers to shoot him. After firing a shot toward the perimeter officers, the suspect retreated to a small wooden shed where another gunshot was heard. The local part-time SWAT team had been requested to respond; however, most of the team members were coming from home. While waiting for SWAT to arrive, command level personnel arrived at the scene and were briefed on the situation. Instead of waiting for the SWAT team to arrive, the command personnel assumed that the last gunshot was the suspect committing suicide and approached the wooden shed in an attempt to see the suspect. As they did, the suspect fired again, narrowly missing both officers. The suspect had not committed suicide and was waiting in ambush for the officers. Luckily, neither officer was injured, and the suspect eventually surrendered to the SWAT team and hostage negotiators.

In other instances, instead of calling and waiting for SWAT to arrive, the quick action of patrol officers could have saved the lives of innocent civilians. On July 18, 1984, a suspect walked into a McDonald's restaurant in San Ysidro, California, and opened fire with three weapons, including an Uzi semi-automatic rifle. During the assault, which lasted 77 minutes, the suspect killed 21 people and wounded an additional 19. Patrol officers were on the scene within 3 minutes of being dispatched to the ongoing shooting and had the entire building surrounded in 15 minutes. As they surrounded the building and waited for the SWAT team to arrive, they listened as the suspect fired a total of 257 rounds. Finally, some 77 minutes after the attack began, a SWAT sniper shot and killed the suspect from a nearby rooftop (*The San Diego Union Times* 1984).

During the era of specialization, what little tactical training was received by patrol officers was typically given by SWAT team members. These instructors often only reinforced the role of patrol first responders as being to contain an incident and call SWAT to handle it. While sound, tactical decision-making skills coupled with actual tactics would have been the ideal blend of training for patrol officers, this was usually not the case. Whether due to an instructor's ego, lack of confidence in the patrol officers, or the belief that this type of training would make the SWAT role irrelevant, very little training involving tactical decision making and skills for patrol officers occurred during the specialization era.

Tactical operations are historically a very slow process from start to finish. Whether it is a callout in the middle of the night to respond to an armed, barricaded gunman or a high-risk warrant served on the date and time determined by the SWAT commander, tactical operations are generally slow and deliberate. Using a nighttime, barricaded gunman as an example, patrol officers, who are first on the scene, must quickly assess the situation and determine whether it meets established criteria for activating the SWAT team. Once notified, SWAT personnel must respond from either home or on-duty assignments. Once on scene, equipment must be donned, briefings conducted, intelligence gathered, and, finally, tactical personnel deployed to relieve on-scene patrol officers. Depending upon the area and time of day, this process can take as little as 30 minutes or as much as several hours.

Once tactical command has been established during a critical incident, traditional tactical methods involving time and patience generally drive the pace of the event. Intelligence gathering and analysis is an important part of any tactical operation and often takes a significant amount of time and resources if done thoroughly and properly. Unfortunately, the intelligence "process" often bogs down decision making and stalls initiative. Over time, many SWAT teams become conditioned to a slow, methodical response protocol, finding themselves unable to work or uncomfortable working in dynamic, quickly changing environments such as an active shooter event.

The Turning Point

On April 20, 1999, at Columbine High School in Littleton, Colorado, two deranged students initiated a long-planned attack on their school. Using rifles, shotguns, and homemade improvised explosive devices (IEDs), the suspects forever changed the way patrol officers and other first responders would respond to ongoing, immediately life-threatening incidents. This phenomenon, ultimately termed an "active shooter" event, was not the first. Although there had been numerous similar active shooter events since the creation of SWAT teams in the early 1970s, none garnered the attention of the law enforcement profession and nation as did the attack on Columbine High School.

Located in suburban Jefferson County, Colorado, Columbine High School is considered an upper-middle class, suburban school. With an enrollment of 2,000 students, the school had 75 classrooms throughout 250,000 square feet of space. There were 120 teachers on faculty and an additional 20 staff members. The school was one of many high schools in the Jefferson County School District, which had a total of 144 schools. At the time of the event, the Jefferson County Sheriff's Office had one deputy, Neil Gardner, assigned full time to the school as a school resource officer (Report of Governor Bill Owens' Columbine Review Commission 2001).

After a year of planning and acquiring the weapons to assault their high school, the two suspects initiated their attack at lunchtime on April 19, 1999. After rigging their vehicles with IEDs, the pair carried two additional large IEDs, created out of propane tanks with timers, into the school's cafeteria and set them near pillars in an attempt to collapse the second floor library onto the cafeteria. Their plan was to wait outside in ambush positions and shoot surviving students who ran from the school after the explosion. When the bombs failed to detonate at 11:17 as programmed, the suspects started shooting students outside the school at 11:19, initiating one of the worst school shootings in history (Jefferson County Sheriff's Office Official Report on Columbine 2000).

School resource officer Neil Gardner, who had been eating lunch in his patrol car near the school, was the first to arrive after receiving a radio call of a "female down in the south lot of Columbine High School." As Gardner pulled into the south parking lot of the school at 11:24, he observed kids running out of the school in every direction as well as smoke coming from the west end of the parking lot. Additionally, he heard the sounds of several loud explosions and gunshots coming from inside the school. As he stepped out of his vehicle, Gardner came under fire from one of the suspects, who was standing on the steps outside the school. The shots, believed to have been fired from a 9mm rifle, missed Gardner. Gardner fired four shots from his duty pistol at the suspect from a distance of approximately 60 yards. Although initially believed to be struck by one of Gardner's rounds, the suspect quickly began shooting again at Gardner before entering the school and passing out of Gardner's sight.

For the next 40 minutes, the two suspects terrorized their classmates and teachers at Columbine High School with gunfire and IEDs. Law enforcement officers from around the Denver metro area responded to the scene to find unbelievable destruction and ongoing violence. Focusing primarily on securing a perimeter, rescuing wounded students outside the school, and escorting uninjured, fleeing students to safety, these officers were responding as they had been trained and conditioned. Although several officers shot at or exchanged gunfire with the two suspects from outside during this time, none entered or attempted to enter the school in pursuit of the gunmen shooting innocent people there. SWAT had been called and this was a situation that a SWAT team should handle under the existing protocols.

During this time, numerous SWAT team members from local agencies began arriving at the school. At 11:52, Jefferson County Undersheriff John Dunaway arrived at the command post and authorized SWAT to make an immediate entry into the school. Initially, 12 SWAT officers from three different agencies created an ad hoc team and were the first law enforcement officers to enter the school. This team was eventually followed by numerous other SWAT elements that entered the school at various times during the event. Working in coordination with each other, the teams fought past unexploded IEDs, waded through ankle deep water from sprinkler systems, worked with deafening fire alarms, and breached locked doors in an attempt to locate the suspects. As the teams searched the school, they encountered students and staff hiding in every imaginable space and then helped them safely exit the school. Finally, at approximately 15:30, the two suspects were found in the school library—dead from self-inflicted gunshot wounds. Although law enforcement did not know it at that moment, these were the only two suspects involved in the attack. The investigation into the Columbine High School massacre would go on for months and years to follow.

A lesson quickly learned from Columbine was that first responding law enforcement officers play a critical role during active shooter situations. Looking back historically since the creation of SWAT teams, the law enforcement profession had conditioned the patrol function to fail in an active shooter situation like Columbine. Not only was there very little or no tactical training provided to patrol officers to respond to this type of event, but also what training was provided reinforced the concept of containment and calling for SWAT teams to handle critical situations. It was very easy to sit back and critique the first responders to Columbine and blame them for not chasing the suspects into the school to end the attack sooner; however, we must not overlook the fact that they were not trained to do this and, more importantly, they were specifically trained *not* to do this. The law enforcement profession finally woke up and collectively agreed that

1. Some critical situations cannot wait for SWAT.
2. First responders (i.e., patrol officers) need tactical training to address ongoing, life-threatening incidents like an active shooter.
3. First responders must be empowered through training, policy and procedure, and equipment to swiftly and effectively respond to and stop an active shooter.

New Response Protocols

In the wake of lessons learned from the police response to Columbine, many law enforcement agencies across the United States began providing active shooter training to patrol officers and other first responders. The training generally consisted of providing basic, SWAT-type tactical training to patrol officers. This approach required existing or former SWAT team members to provide the training. In theory, this practice made sense. Tactical officers are an agency's subject matter experts in tactics and firearms. The tactical skills that patrol officers needed to respond to and address an active shooter threat are basically the aggressive, small-unit tactics on which SWAT teams were founded. In many agencies, SWAT officers also held collateral duties as training officers and had extensive experience in teaching police officers. For agencies with full-time SWAT teams, SWAT personnel often had the time to conduct training and could be easily loaned to the training division. Finally, almost all SWAT team members came from patrol divisions and had experience with the patrol job and function.

Although this ultimately proved to be a successful model for training patrol personnel for active shooter response, it was not without challenges and failures. One of the first challenges many experienced SWAT instructors had to overcome when teaching patrol officers was to deflate their (the trainers') often large egos and sense of superiority over patrol officers. Special units like SWAT teams require a certain "esprit de corps" to be successful. Unfortunately, this attitude and mentality can be detrimental when interacting with groups or persons outside those units. Police instructors, no matter what their background, must understand that the mission of imparting knowledge and teaching life-saving skills takes precedence over their individual perception of self-worth and importance. A specific instructional style that may work very well for teaching new SWAT team recruits frequently turns off the 15- or 20-year patrol veteran who has no interest in doing anything "tactical." Unfortunately, these are the frontline officers who most need training in dealing with active shooters.

Another challenge facing SWAT instructors is the need to transition often complex, complicated tactics into easy-to-use and easy-to-remember responses for officers with no tactical experience. Traditional SWAT tactics are built upon small, fixed teams with specific responsibilities for each team member. These team members work together and train together, frequently spending inordinate amounts of time honing specific skill sets that can be performed under extreme stress. However, the training required for patrol officers to respond to an active shooter event focuses on the ability of the first responding officers, no matter who they work for or what uniform they are wearing, to work together to stop an active shooter swiftly and effectively. Complex tactics relying on fixed teams, fellow responders who are known and trusted, and the need for strict training regimens to hone skills are ineffective training methodologies for the patrol response to an active shooter.

SWAT team members who train patrol officers are also confronted with the need to transition from tactical philosophies and methodologies that dictate hard, structured response protocols to more fluid and dynamic decision-making processes in the moment. For example, most tactical teams deploy flashbangs or flash-sound diversionary devices prior to entering a crisis site to stun and disorient suspects temporarily. Additionally, when searching for and clearing a structure of suspects, SWAT teams work methodically, searching and clearing as they go without any chance of missing a suspect that could come up behind the team. Finally, tactical teams have specialized equipment including breaching tools, shields, and weapons-mounted tactical lights. Specific tactics used by these teams are often gear dependent; that is, without a shield or a certain tool, the tactics used to address a situation will not work or will be ineffective.

For active shooter tactical training targeted at first responders to be effective, police trainers, including SWAT personnel assigned to train patrol officers in these new tactics, had to rethink and adjust traditional training methodologies. First, patrol personnel receive little tactical training and, depending upon the size of the agency, will likely receive active shooter training only once or twice during their careers. Police instructors generally have between 4 and 16 hours to provide this critical training. If the tactics are too complex to learn in this limited amount of time, patrol officers will become frustrated and have no confidence in the tactics. Therefore, the training must be concept and principle based, easy to learn, and even easier to recall and use under extreme stress.

Secondly, the response protocols and tactics taught to patrol personnel could not be identical to traditional SWAT tactics. Patrol officers who respond to an active shooter event will not have a ballistic shield in their patrol car that can be instantly deployed. These officers are not trained in or equipped to use flashbangs. They generally do not carry forced breaching tools, such as rams or pry bars, and have not been trained to use a shotgun to breach a locked door. The mission that patrol officers are being prepared to conduct—a worst-case hostage rescue in an active shooter event—is the same mission SWAT teams train for every day. However, patrol officers are being tasked with doing the mission with little or no training, no specialized equipment, and extremely limited previous intelligence on the situation. The tactics utilized in these situations must be dynamic, aggressive, and decisive, and this is counter to much of the patrol officer's previous training regarding this type of situation.

Additionally, active shooter training for patrol must be designed to enable several officers who may never have worked together before, do not know each other, and are possibly from different agencies to come together and effectively respond to stop the violence. The patrol division in virtually every law enforcement agency contains personnel with wide-ranging tenure, experience, and backgrounds. As seen at the Columbine High School tragedy, the radio call for an ongoing active shooter situation will bring a swift response from police officers throughout the area. The most important of these responders are the first several on the scene, who are tasked with locating, isolating, and neutralizing the ongoing threat. The training, then, must not be dependent on a homogenous, dedicated group of responders, but instead a concept and principle-based program enabling any officer to step up and be an effective member of an emergency ad hoc team. It should be noted here that in active shooter scenarios, this is the ultimate goal: to neutralize the ongoing threat and stop the killing as quickly as possible.

Dynamic force-on-force, scenario-based training, which had historically been reserved for SWAT team type of training, must also be incorporated and used to prepare patrol personnel. Many agencies wrongly believe police officers can be adequately trained to stop an active shooter by sitting through a PowerPoint presentation or conducting table-top exercises. Although this type of training can be valuable to raise awareness, it often does very little to actually prepare an officer to step out of the patrol vehicle and enter a crisis site while shots are being fired.

Force-on-force training for law enforcement was relatively new at the time of the Columbine shootings. This type of training, which involves scenario-based exercises where officers actually fire nonlethal projectiles such as paintballs and other developing technologies, was primarily restricted to tactical team training. The training required dedicated training venues and extensive safety protocols, and could be expensive to conduct. However, if done properly, this training is arguably the best method actually to teach and then assess outcomes of tactical training. In order to build successful patrol response capabilities, this type of hands-on training must be incorporated into all active shooter training programs.

Finally, and possibly most importantly, a new paradigm in crisis decision making, specifically at the first-line supervisor and midlevel management tiers of police agencies, had to be implemented. Looking back to the traditional patrol response procedures used prior to Columbine, all tactical maneuvers and interventions usually had to be authorized by the highest levels of the police agency. In an active shooter event, there is no time to wait for supervisor and command approvals to enter a structure and stop the killing of innocent victims. A new decision-making matrix for crisis situations that could be implemented at the lowest levels of an organization had to be developed.

Patrol personnel and other first responders had to be empowered to make immediate life-saving decisions in active shooter events. With this empowerment also comes training; however, training must also be provided to the supervisors and managers who are relinquishing the decision-making authority. This fundamental change in traditional law enforcement management challenges long-held assumptions and practices. Fear of litigation, lack of trust in the capabilities of the patrol officers, and difficulty in decentralized control during a crisis continue to plague the law enforcement profession. However, for a swift and effective patrol response to the ongoing killing of innocent victims to work, those first responders must be empowered and have the authority to make immediate decisions without waiting for permission from commanders and chiefs back at the station.

Just as the tactics taught to patrol officers responding to an active shooter need to be flexible, the response strategies employed by supervisors and managers to one of these critical events need to be flexible as well. In some agencies, an active shooter event was only declared if first responding officers could hear ongoing gunshots. Absent ongoing gunshots, the more traditional "containment and call SWAT" response protocol for patrol officers was deemed the appropriate response. Every tactical situation in law enforcement is different and a "one size fits all" response strategy is not appropriate. However, fundamental professional law enforcement principles such as the preservation of life, protecting the innocent from predators, and performing duties as prescribed in the Law Enforcement Code of Ethics must be the driving force behind tactical decisions made during times of crisis (Institute for Criminal Justice Ethics 1991).

An example of limitations forced on first responders by hard-and-fast policy directives occurred on Friday, April 3, 2009, in Binghamton, New York. At approximately 10:30 a.m., a suspect parked his car at the rear of a building housing the American Civic Association Immigration Center in downtown Binghamton. The suspect strategically parked his car blocking the rear door to the building so that it could not be opened from the inside. The suspect then entered the front door to the clinic, immediately shot two receptionists, and continued into the building randomly shooting people attending an ESL (English as a second language) course.

A wounded receptionist retreated under a desk and immediately called 911 to report the shooting. Patrol officers arrived on the scene within 2 minutes of the first 911 calls; however, an immediate entry into the building was not conducted. When the suspect heard sirens outside the building, he fatally shot himself in the head. In the approximate 3-minute attack, the suspect fired 99 shots: 88 from a 9mm handgun and 11 from a .45 caliber handgun. He had killed 13 victims and wounded 2 before killing himself.

The patrol officers, responding to the report of shots fired and a victim shot inside the building, did not hear any more shots being fired when they arrived at 10:33 a.m. The wounded receptionist, who stayed on 911 during the entire event until she was eventually rescued, provided intelligence information indicating the shooting had stopped. At approximately 10:37 a.m., the SWAT team was requested to respond. According to the American Civic Association after-Action Report and Improvement Plan commissioned by Broome County (2009) after the event, "Police remained outside the building until confirmation that the shooter and any potential accomplices were dead." SWAT team members entered the building at 11:13 a.m., approximately 40 minutes after the first officers arrived, and ultimately escorted 10 survivors from the building at noon and 10 more at 12:40 p.m. (Beck Disaster Recovery 2009).

Police officials responsible for the tactical strategies employed at the American Civic Association tragedy believed the response into the building was one that "warranted caution" since they were unsure if the suspect was still alive or not (Kekis 2009). Although they were being fed real-time intelligence from a wounded victim near the entry point of the building, the officials chose to "be more deliberate because the gunman had stopped firing by the time they arrived" (Kekis 2009). The officials added, "He was dead. We didn't know it. If there's a bunch of cops laying [*sic*] on the floor [who have been] shot trying to rescue somebody else, it's not going to help anybody." The officials stated without question that officers would have gone into the building "if shots had still been flying" (Kekis 2009).

The police response in Binghamton again created questions and debate over the role of first responders to an active shooter event. Training and response protocols would be very easy to instruct, recall, and initiate if real-life tactical situations were black and white with a corresponding "playbook" of responses. Unfortunately, real-world situations are dynamic, fluid events, often changing drastically due to the human element. To assist with decision making under stress during these situations, law enforcement uses a theory of "life safety." This theory applies not only to actions and responses driving law enforcement to act, such as a victim needing rescue, but also to the "life safety" of those doing the rescue. These conflicting interests are magnified in an active shooter situation since there is no safe way to enter a structure and confront a deranged gunman randomly shooting people or to rescue those who have already been wounded.

To assist law enforcement officers, supervisors, and managers with decision making during critical, life-threatening events, a "priority of life" scale has been developed. In order of importance, the scale is

1. Innocent civilians, hostages, and victims
2. Police officers
3. Suspects

When first introduced to the priority of life scale, many law enforcement professionals quickly argue, as was done by the Binghamton police officials, that police officers do no one any good if they become casualties themselves. In essence this argument concludes that the lives of police officers must take precedence over those of innocent victims in order for those same victims or potential victims to be saved. Using this reasoning, the only completely safe location for police officers responding to an active shooter event is outside the structure where the shooting is occurring. By entering the building in search of a gunman targeting innocents, police officers are actually placing themselves second on the priority of life scale behind those innocent civilians.

Modern day active shooter training standards and tactical philosophies do not suggest officers run into active shooter situations with complete disregard for their personal safety. To the contrary, officers today generally are better trained, equipped, and prepared to face a violent adversary than ever before. Wearing body armor and being armed, often with patrol rifles, officers are much better prepared to confront and stop an active shooter than the innocent civilians being hunted. When put into context and explained in this manner, professional law enforcement officers understand the concept that although their safety is important, the policing profession can be and is a dangerous calling that sometimes requires those who have sworn an oath to step up and be the "thin blue line" charged with protecting those who cannot protect themselves. In the next chapter, we discuss the increasing complexity and terrorist aspects of active shooter events.

References

Broome County American Civic Association. September 2009. Shooting, April 3, 2009. After-action report & improvement plan. Beck Disaster Recovery. http://content.news10now.com/syrcontent/pdfs/484312_Broome_County_ACA_Shooting_After_Action_Report.pdf (retrieved September 7, 2012).

Institute for Criminal Justice Ethics. 1991. Law enforcement code of ethics (rev.). http://www.lib.jjay.cuny.edu/cje/html/codes/codes-usa-organizational/lece-r.html (retrieved September 7, 2012).

Jefferson County Sheriff's Office Official Report on Columbine. May 15, 2000. http://denver.rockymountainnews.com/shooting/report/columbinereport/pages/toc.htm (retrieved August 20, 2012).

Kekis, J. 2009. N.Y. officials defend police response to massacre, April 6, 2009, Policeone.com, http://www.policeone.com/active-shooter/articles/1807053-N-Y-officials-defend-police-response-to-massacre/ (retrieved September 7, 2012).

Mijares, T., R. McCarthy, and D. Perkins. 2000. *The management of police specialized tactical units*. Springfield, IL: Charles C Thomas Publisher, LTD.

Report of Governor Bill Owens' Columbine Review Commission. May 2001. http://www.state.co.us/columbine/Columbine_20Report_WEB.pdf (retrieved August 20, 2012).

The San Diego Union-Tribune. A massacre in San Ysidro. http://www.utsandiego.com/san-ysidro-massacre (retrieved August 19, 2012).

S.W.A.T. Internet Movie Database (www.IMDb.com), http://www.
imdb.com/title/tt0072560/plotsummary (retrieved August 19,
2012).

Walker, S. and Katz, C. 2005. *The Police in America: An
Introduction.* New York: McGraw-Hill.

Chapter 2

Increased Complexity of Events

Introduction

There are numerous reasons why deranged suspects engage in an active shooter attack. Whether due to mental illness, the loss of a job, a perceived injustice, political motivations, or other causes, these suspects all have one goal: to kill and injure as many victims as possible before being stopped by authorities. Several active shooters appear to have reviewed the strengths and weaknesses of previous attacks carefully in an attempt to increase the number of people who are killed. This careful planning has led to attacks that dramatically increase the complexity of the events and make effective law enforcement response much more difficult.

For example, on April 16, 2007, a student at Virginia Tech University murdered 32 and injured 17 students and faculty in two related incidents on the campus. At approximately 7:10 a.m., the suspect first shot and killed two students in West Ambler-Johnston Hall, a dormitory the shooter did not live in and had no known connection to. At approximately 9:40 a.m., the suspect attacked and shot students attending classes in

Norris Hall, a typical college classroom building. Law enforcement officers arrived at Norris Hall within minutes of the suspect beginning his attack, and shortly after their arrival, the suspect shot and killed himself, ending the worst school shooting in US history (Giduck and Chi 2008; Report of the Virginia Tech Review Panel 2007). The shooter did several things that dramatically increased the complexity of the police response to this event. These actions are discussed next.

The Virginia Polytechnic Institute and State University, known as Virginia Tech University (VT), is located in the town of Blacksburg, Virginia. Approximately 40 miles southwest of Roanoke, Virginia, Blacksburg is a university-oriented community with a population of approximately 40,000 residents. Due to the university, the typical daytime population surges to over 70,000 with students, university employees, and visitors commuting into Blacksburg. The university has a student population of more than 28,000 with approximately 9,000 residing on campus. There are 7,133 university employees (Giduck and Chi 2008).

The campus consists of more than 2,600 acres with 125 major buildings and an airport. There are 16 road entrances to campus leading to more than 19 miles of roads. None are controlled by gates or guarded stations. The Division I school boasts numerous state-of-the-art athletic facilities including Lane Stadium/Worsham Field, which has a capacity of 65,632 (Virginia Tech University website).

The Virginia Tech Police Department (VTPD) had an authorized strength of 40 officers and was led by Chief Wendell Flinchum at the time of the attacks. During weekdays, VTPD had 14 officers on duty including 5 officers on patrol and 9 officers working office hours. Since 1991, the VTPD has had an 8- to 10-person tactical team, a volunteer assignment that is a collateral duty with strict selection and training criteria. The tactical team has specialized training and equipment consistent with industry standards for tactical teams across the nation (Giduck and Chi 2008).

The Blacksburg Police Department (BPD), led by Chief Kim Crannis, had an authorized strength of 57 officers. All BPD patrol officers were issued patrol rifles and received training in both rifles and shotguns, including shotgun breaching. BPD had a 13 member part-time tactical team, created after 9/11, as well. The VTPD and BPD tactical teams trained together monthly and routinely deployed together on actual call-ups. Unfortunately, the two agencies did not share a common radio channel and historically communicated using cellular phones and Nextel Direct Connect during operations (Giduck and Chi 2008).

All members of the BPD and the VTPD had participated in joint active shooter training prior to April 2007. As recently as 2 months prior to the April attack, both departments' tactical teams conducted an active shooter training exercise at a local middle school. In addition, both agencies had conducted joint terrorist attack response and mass casualty training prior to the 2007 attack (Giduck and Chi 2008).

The police response to the active shooter in Norris Hall was nothing short of a textbook example of lessons learned from Columbine. It remains unknown to this day why the suspect murdered the two students in West Ambler-Johnston Hall hours before beginning his killing spree at Norris Hall. If it was to create a diversion and draw law enforcement resources away from being able to respond to Norris Hall, it actually had just the opposite effect. Two very forward-thinking police administrators, Chief Crannis and Chief Flinchum, recognizing they had a very uncommon violent crime for their community and marshaled both agencies' tactical resources immediately after the discovery of the murder victims in West Ambler-Johnston. This response strategy more than doubled the number of officers that were available to respond when the shooting started in Norris Hall. In addition, the officers who had been called in were tactical officers, specially trained in many tactical skills, including shotgun breaching, which would become critical in the response to Norris Hall (Giduck and Chi 2008).

The SWAT team members and off-duty personnel who had been recalled to work after the initial discovery of two victims were assigned various duties including scene security and roving patrols. The SWAT team members were paired up in patrol vehicles to increase immediate deployment capabilities as well as communication between agencies, and staged at West Ambler-Johnston Hall and the Blacksburg Police Department. Additional SWAT team members were performing collateral duties as they were on duty at the time of the initial call and were performing their primary jobs as detectives and patrol officers (Giduck and Chi 2008).

At approximately 9:15 a.m., the suspect entered Norris Hall and began chaining and locking the three exterior, public access doors. On one of the doors, the suspect placed a handwritten note claiming that if the chains and lock were removed, a bomb would go off. A staff member located the note just prior to the suspect starting to shoot on the second floor; however, police were not immediately notified and the shooting started only minutes later (Giduck and Chi 2008). It was later learned that this staff member took the note to a supervisor instead of immediately notifying the police. At approximately 9:41 a.m., the suspect started shooting his fellow students and professors in room 206.

Law enforcement officers were on the scene at Norris Hall within 3 minutes of the first 911 call (Report of the Virginia Tech Review Panel 2007). More than a dozen officers, including Chiefs Crannis and Flinchum, could hear the ongoing gunshots coming from Norris Hall as they separated into three teams and moved to three different breach points (Giduck and Chi 2008; Report of the Virginia Tech Review Panel 2007). At least eight of these officers were SWAT team members who had been called in after the first shootings. This quick response to get into the crisis site was not by accident. It came from training and lessons learned from previous tragedies, including Columbine. However, a new tactical dilemma faced the first responders as they pulled on the doors to enter the building and stop the ongoing killing.

Each of the three exterior doors the officers were attempting to enter had been chained and locked shut by the suspect. This action not only prevented law enforcement from entering the building, but it also prevented victims from being able to escape the gunfire. Once finding the doors were chained, two of the teams combined into a single entry team and immediately transitioned to another door to gain entry. Upon discovering this door was also chained, an attempt to breach the chain with a shotgun was made; however, the breach was unsuccessful. These officers then moved to another nearby maintenance door where they were able to use a shotgun effectively to breach the lock. Once inside Norris Hall, the officers were immediately able to determine the shots had been coming from the second floor. The teams split up again and tactically moved to the second floor in search of the gunman. At this point, the suspect had already committed suicide (Giduck and Chi 2008; Report of the Virginia Tech Review Panel 2007).

Based on the visual carnage of the wounded and dead on the second floor of Norris Hall, the officers believed there must have been more than one suspect. With no more shots being heard and before determining the known threat was down, some officers began rescuing the wounded and placing them in secure areas where tactical medics assigned to both agencies' SWAT teams could begin life-saving treatment. Minutes after reaching the second floor, the officers did locate the suspect, dead from a self-inflicted gunshot wound to his head, in room 211. Still believing there must have been more than one suspect, the officers began a simultaneous process of searching the building for additional threats, establishing security for the wounded and tactical medics working on them, and evacuating the wounded out of the building. Ultimately, every victim who was alive when removed from Norris Hall would survive (Giduck and Chi 2008; Report of the Virginia Tech Review Panel 2007).

As with every active shooter event, lessons can and should be learned. One of the lessons from Virginia Tech was the need for first responders, specifically patrol personnel, to have a breaching capability. By simply chaining and locking the entrance doors, the suspect was able to slow down the police entry into the building. In this case, many of the first responders were actually SWAT team members who were trained and equipped for shotgun breaching. If this had not been the case at Norris Hall, one can only imagine how many more victims could have been shot and killed before officers could gain entry into the building. Manual and shotgun breaching capabilities for patrol personnel, unheard of prior to the attacks at Virginia Tech, are now becoming training standards throughout the country. With proper training and equipment, patrol officers who find themselves arriving first on the scene of the next active shooter event should be capable of forcing entry into a barricaded structure to stop the killing and save lives.

Another important lesson from the tragedy at Virginia Tech was the critical roles the tactical medics from each agency's SWAT team played in saving lives. Emergency medical service (EMS) and other specially trained medical personnel will be responding to an active shooter event; however, current protocols prohibit these emergency personnel from entering a crisis site before law enforcement is able to secure the site. As was witnessed at Virginia Tech, as well as Columbine, the crisis site may not be completely secure for hours as law enforcement methodically clears the structure to ensure the threat has in fact been eliminated. Law enforcement officers need to have basic, life-saving medical training, similar to the training members of our armed forces receive before deploying overseas. This would enable any police officer, not just tactical medics assigned to SWAT teams, to be able to provide aid immediately to critically injured victims before EMS is able to reach the victims.

The critical role of training, working together, and preplanning for critical incidents before a tragic event was clearly demonstrated at Virginia Tech. The law enforcement community in Blacksburg, Virginia, knew how to respond appropriately on April 16, 2007. They had worked together for years, trained together for active shooter events, and the leadership from both agencies was progressive and forward thinking. Positive law enforcement interagency working relationships do not happen overnight and are not created without challenges and great leadership. The preexisting and established partnerships between the Virginia Tech University Police Department and the Blacksburg Police Department clearly led to a successful law enforcement response to the tragedy that could have been much, much worse.

In the end, one of the many things Virginia Tech taught us is that law enforcement can do virtually everything correctly and, yet, a committed perpetrator can still cause the deadliest school shooting in our nation's history. However, this fact cannot be allowed to discourage or dissuade law enforcement officers, especially the true first responders, from being properly trained, equipped, and empowered to step up to stop an active shooter.

Another active shooter event that challenged existing training standards occurred at Fort Hood, Texas, on November 5, 2009. At approximately 1:30 p.m., a US Army officer entered the Soldier Readiness Center and began shooting unarmed soldiers and civilians. First responding civilian law enforcement officers from the Fort Hood Department of Emergency Services, Sergeants Mark Todd and Kim Munley, arrived within 3 minutes of the first 911 call and located the suspect outside the building as he continued to fire on innocent victims. Both officers engaged the suspect with gunfire and Sergeant Munley was critically wounded in the firefight. The suspect was shot, immobilized, and taken into custody. A total of 13 people were killed and 43 others were wounded or injured (III Corps and Fort Hood 05 Nov 09 after Action Review, 2009;

Protecting the Force: Lessons from Fort Hood, Report of the DoD Independent Review 2010).

Most domestic active shooter events have occurred inside structures including malls, schools, churches, and businesses (Kelly 2011). In the case at Fort Hood, the suspect began his assault in a building, but went mobile and transitioned to walking outside the building while continuing to hunt and shoot victims. The first two officers on the scene actually encountered and engaged the suspect outdoors. Traditional active shooter training and tactics have focused on interior movements and common SWAT close-quarter battle (CQB) tactics. Some active shooter training programs and curricula, including the Advanced Law Enforcement Rapid Response Training (ALERRT) Program at Texas State University-San Marcos, actually teach exterior movement techniques for patrol officers and other first responders. Although the tactical objective remains the same in both environments (to stop the killing), specific tactics to accomplish the mission are very different. Traditional tactics learned and used to combat an active shooter inside a structure are ineffective and unsound when confronting an adversary in an exterior, open environment. Fortunately for the first responders at Fort Hood, they had been trained through the ALERRT program and credit this training with their swift and effective response (Protecting the Force: Lessons from Fort Hood, Report of the DoD Independent Review 2010).

Yet another event that presented first responders with new complexities occurred on Friday, July 30, 2012, during the premier of the movie *The Dark Knight Rises* at a movie theater in Aurora, Colorado. A lone gunman entered theater number nine at approximately 12:38 a.m. and began one of the worst mass shootings in US history. The suspect, who had propped open an exterior fire exit door, entered the theater while the movie was playing and threw what has been described as a tear gas canister or smoke grenade into the crowd. During the ensuing chaos of the movie playing and the smoke, the suspect opened fire on the crowded theater with a rifle and a shotgun. By the end of the assault, 12 innocent persons had been killed and another 58 were wounded (Bustillo, Banjo, and Audi 2012; Garrett 2012).

First responding law enforcement officers were overwhelmed with people trying to escape the theater, many of whom were wounded. Within the first 6 minutes, officers located the suspect at the rear of the theater near his vehicle. The suspect was dressed in police equipment, which looked very similar to SWAT team gear (i.e., wearing body armor, a Kevlar helmet, and a gas mask). He was taken into custody without further incident and numerous weapons were seized (Bustillo et al. 2012; Garrett 2012).

The shootings in Aurora again highlight the critical role law enforcement first responders have in treating and processing the wounded in a mass casualty event. Officers repeatedly called for medics, ambulances, and fire-rescue personnel to assist with the dozens of wounded victims (*The Denver Post* 2012). Unfortunately, very few, if any, EMS organizations in the country, and certainly not the EMS system in Aurora, Colorado, are capable of handling a mass casualty event with more than 50 gunshot victims without mutual aid and assistance. Notifying and coordinating a mutual aid medical response of this magnitude takes valuable time and, while this is occurring, victims are potentially dying. Law enforcement officers need to be trained in hemorrhage control, the use of tourniquets, casualty collection, and triage. This basic medical training, consistent with the training our armed forces personnel receive, should be the new training standard just as active shooter training was after Columbine.

The Terrorist Active Shooter Threat

Unfortunately, the active shooter threat facing our nation's first responders does not only lie within the borders of the

United States. Terrorist organizations around the globe have recognized and identified the small-arms, active shooter attack model as a viable tool to be used against a civilized society. Organized terrorist groups have not only attacked hotels, shopping centers, mass transit stations, and places of worship with the active shooter tactic, but also schools, killing hundreds of children in furtherance of their ideological and political goals. Some of the most violent groups in the world are conducting active shooter attacks on innocent civilians only miles from the Texas border in Mexico. American law enforcement officers, managers, and trainers must recognize this increasing threat and be prepared to respond swiftly and effectively to any active shooter event whether domestically motivated or born from and conducted by terrorists.

The post-Columbine law enforcement era saw a drastic change in preparedness measures and capabilities of patrol officers who would find themselves responding to an active shooter event. Most police training academies introduced some type of active shooter training program, even if it was only a PowerPoint awareness-level briefing. Because several high-profile active shooter events occurred at schools, many agencies and police trainers unfortunately pigeonholed active shooter training as a school violence response issue. In reality, these events occur frequently in the workplace, carried out by disgruntled employees and former employees (Kelly 2011). The initial police response to an active shooter, no matter where the event is occurring, should be consistent and focused on stopping the killing of innocent persons.

As the active shooter phenomenon became more prevalent in the media after Columbine, postevent research showed several common trends emerging regarding all active shooter events; most are carried out by lone gunmen and they often commit suicide (Kelly 2011 and see Chapter 3). Many police agencies and trainers, looking only at the statistics from previous events, structured their active shooter training to represent only what had occurred in the past. However, in the post-9/11 world, a new active shooter threat emerged. Organized terrorist organizations such as Al-Qaeda and Lashkar-e-Taiba (LeT) quickly seized on the simplicity and effectiveness of the small-arms active shooter attack model, creating a new threat to America (Nye 2008). For some agencies, old training methodologies would again need to be revamped to prepare first responders for an adversary who would not only kill as many innocent persons as possible, but also fight to the death. Next we discuss several of the best known small-arms terrorist attacks and their implications for active shooter training in the United States.

Beslan, Russia

Beslan, Russia is an agricultural and industrial community situated 900 miles south of Moscow. With a population of approximately 40,000, the town is small, poor, and home to the region's largest vodka factory (Giduck 2005). On September 1, 2004, the traditional first day of school for children in Russia, a community celebration was taking place at the Beslan Middle School. That morning, entire families escorted their children to school for a traditional celebration known as "Day of Knowledge" to celebrate the children's first day of school (Giduck 2005). Tragically, at approximately 9:05 a.m., 49 terrorists assaulted the celebration, taking 1,181 hostages after killing a police officer and security guard (Giduck 2005). The terrorists, primarily from Eastern Bloc countries near Russia, would ultimately hold the hostages for 62 hours, killing many of them during this time (Giduck 2005).

Law enforcement officials in Beslan were completely untrained and unprepared to respond to a crisis of this magnitude. Even had the local police forces mounted an initial assault in an attempt to repel the attack, the sheer number of terrorists, along with the weapons they used, would likely have made any type of counterassault a catastrophic failure. The inability of the Russian police forces to stop the initial assault enabled the terrorists to control the school completely, create defensive positions, and set up booby traps and explosives to prevent a future assault on the school (Giduck 2005). By the time Russian Special Forces—who would ultimately conduct the hostage rescue in an attempt to end the siege on the third day—arrived, the school had been transformed into a fortress of explosives occupied by heavily armed terrorists willing to die for their cause.

On September 3, 2004, a brutal and fierce battle between the terrorists and Russian Special Forces commenced in an effort to rescue the hundreds of hostages being held in deplorable conditions. In a battle that lasted for hours, 330 hostages were killed, 172 of those children, and 700 were reported as wounded (Giduck 2005). Twenty-one Russian soldiers gave their lives during the rescue attempt, many shot from behind by civilians who were shooting at the school in an attempt to help during the assault (Giduck 2005). Although discrepancies exist in the exact number of terrorists that were killed during the rescue, it is believed that 31 of the original 49 terrorists were killed during the battle, but only 17 of those were eventually identified (Giduck 2005).

Beslan, Russia is thousands of miles away from the shores of the United States and many American law enforcement officials are often quick to dismiss terrorist attacks committed abroad, stating, "That could never happen here." Although the attack in Beslan was not a traditional active shooter event as witnessed at Columbine, it was a school takeover by terrorists with the sole mission to kill as many people as possible, just not immediately. Just as law enforcement agencies can learn and adjust tactics from past events, so too can terrorist elements or lone wolf operatives. Al-Qaeda has warned they will kill American children, and terrorist training videos have been seized abroad showing training camps where attacks are being rehearsed on mock schools (Remsberg 2006). An attack on an American school utilizing similar tactics, if only done by a handful of committed terrorists, would be a significant challenge for even the largest of agencies. What would initially appear to be a hostage situation dictating a more traditional patrol response of containment and calling for specialized units would actually be a siege where the terrorists are buying time to fortify and strengthen their position in order to maximize the body count.

This type of attack scenario challenges even post-Columbine patrol response active shooter protocols. In one sense, after the initial assault and seizure of victims, the event will appear as a static, traditional hostage situation. As has been since the development of specialized units, this is a job for a dedicated SWAT team and hostage negotiators. However, once properly identified as such, this type of event is simply a delayed active shooter or mass murder. Using the traditional tactic of "time" and relying on lengthy negotiations to resolve this type of hostage situation will only allow for further fortification of the terrorists' stronghold and make it much harder to assault when necessary. In order to prevent this from occurring, aggressive tactical decisions and interventions must be made quickly against the committed terrorists, even if no shots are being fired or hostages actively being killed. Time is of the essence. Tragically, this scenario will undoubtedly end in the loss of innocent life, including that of police officers. It is not only a lose–lose situation, but also a lose little or lose very big situation. Decisions and actions taken by the first responders will dictate how bad the loss is.

Mumbai, India

A more traditional active shooter style terrorist attack occurred in Mumbai, India on November 26, 2008. Unlike the traditional active shooter attack, this event lasted 62 hours. During the early morning hours on November 26, 10 members of the Lashkar-e-Taiba (LeT) terrorist organization based in Pakistan came ashore at Mumbai Sassoon Dock aboard small inflatable boats (McPartland 2011). The 10 terrorists, each armed with assault rifles, explosives, and hand grenades, split into four teams and spread out across the city of Mumbai. Under the cover of darkness, the teams began attacking "soft targets," randomly shooting victims at will while planting timed explosive charges in taxis. For the next 60 hours, the terrorists held the city hostage while the police and military attempted to gain control of the situation. In the end, 166 citizens were killed, 304 wounded, and many police officers were killed or seriously injured (Duraphe 2009).

Mumbai, formerly known as Bombay, is home to more than 14 million people. The city is a very dense, urban area consisting of 233 square miles. It is the financial and technological center of India, and the port of Mumbai handles approximately one-half of India's cargo traffic. There are 40,000 employees in the Mumbai Police Service. Most police officers are armed only with a baton; however, some weapons are available, including Glock 9mm pistols and Lee-Enfield .303 rifles (McPartland 2011).

The attackers intentionally planned their assault to coincide with the commuter rush hour when they would have the maximum number of victims available. Their ultimate goal was the same commonly seen in domestic active shooter events: to kill and injure as many victims as possible. One team attacked the Leopold Café, firing randomly into the building, throwing grenades and killing 10 civilians. This team made their way to the Taj Mahal Hotel, where they continued the assault, ultimately barricading themselves before being killed by police and military forces some 60 hours after the initial attacks (McPartland 2011; Dehncke 2010).

A second team of terrorists moved on foot to the Nariman House, a commercial–residential complex run by the Jewish Chabad Lubavich movement. The attackers planted improvised explosive devices (IEDs) in and near the complex, creating large explosions while using their AK-47 assault rifles to shoot victims randomly. Nine hostages were ultimately killed during a battle with government forces that used machine guns and rocket propelled grenades to fight the terrorists (McPartland 2011; Dehncke 2010).

The third team of attackers went to the Oberoi Trident Hotel, where they killed 32 victims in the first hour. The remaining two terrorists assaulted the Chhatrapati Shivaji Terminus (CST), a major train station and transportation hub in Mumbai. These two inflicted the most damage, accounting for the deaths of 58 people, including innocent civilians and police officers, in a matter of minutes (McPartland 2011; Dehncke 2010). This same team, upon leaving the CST, attacked the Cama Hospital, randomly shooting victims and throwing hand grenades (Duraphe 2009).

The Mumbai-style attack, referred to as a "complex coordinated attack," is a significant concern to American law enforcement. First, terrorists utilizing this small-arms, active shooter tactic will not be the typical type of suspect that American law enforcement has trained to confront. These suspects will not commit suicide when confronted by law enforcement like many traditional active shooter suspects. These suspects, who will most likely be well trained and equipped, will fight to the death. As witnessed with the 9/11 attackers, these suspects will be committed to their cause and will have already made the decision that they will be killed during the attacks.

Secondly, multiple active shooter events occurring simultaneously in one city or geographic area will strain, if not collapse, local response capabilities. Single active shooter events often challenge local resources, both from the initial response perspective as well as from the command and control viewpoint. Historically, and depending upon the size of the jurisdiction where the active shooter event is occurring, virtually all local and regional law enforcement resources are directed to that one crisis event. In a complex coordinated attack scenario, local and regional resources will have to be directed to multiple events occurring at the same time. Frontline patrol officers and other first responders, if trained appropriately, will be able to combat the ongoing active shooter events. However, the command and control of multiple attacks, including the marshaling and deployment of available resources, will be one of the most challenging aspects of this type of attack. As witnessed in both Beslan and Mumbai, a lack of immediate response to and containment and control of a terrorist attack of this nature only prolongs the incident and increases the loss of innocent life.

Norway

One of the world's most violent active shooter events occurred on July 22, 2011, in the otherwise peaceful country of Norway. A lone gunman, with a domestic terrorist ideology, shook the small country and the world when he first planted a car bomb in downtown Oslo, Norway, and then went on a shooting spree on an isolated island, killing 69 children and wounding an additional 60 (Ergenbright and Hubbard 2012). This tragic attack again featured a deranged gunman using distraction attacks before setting out to attack his primary target as an active shooter. In the Norway case, the suspect also attacked an isolated island, which ultimately made stopping his rampage very difficult due to logistics of gaining access to the crisis site.

With a population of approximately 4.7 million people, Norway is similar in size to New York City, but Norway's violent crime rate is much lower than New York City's. From 2004 to 2009, the number of violent crimes reported per year in Norway did not surpass 25,000 compared to New York City, which recorded over 100,000 major violent felony incidents each year during the same time frame (Ergenbright and Hubbard 2012).

All police services in Norway, outside the special VIP police unit, must obtain permission to arm themselves during the course of their work. The National Counter Terrorism Unit, known as DELTA, must also obtain permission to arm themselves for specific missions around the country. Weapons are easily accessible to the police; however, the practice of requiring command level authorization to arm themselves stands in stark contrast to most police agencies around the world (Ergenbright and Hubbard 2012).

The Norway National Police Directorate has approximately 13,000 peace officers with differing degrees of specialization. All police officers in the country must attend a national police academy, which facilitates common language and standard operations among all police departments (Ergenbright and Hubbard 2012). Similarly to the United States, training is continuing and ongoing throughout an officer's career. According to Ergenbright and Hubbard (2012), although Norwegian police officers receive training on how to interdict and stop an active shooter threat, "Norwegian SOP prefers the skills of the designated National Counter Terrorist unit over the average police officer." However, as was learned from Columbine and other historical active shooter events in the United States, there is often no time to wait for specialized units in an active shooter event.

There are also specialized units within the directorate, including emergency response teams who are trained to manage more complex attacks within their respective districts. The most highly trained, nationally based response team, tasked to counter threats associated with acts of terror, sabotage, hostage situations, and organized crime, is known as the National Counter Terrorism Unit (DELTA). This unit would ultimately be responsible for responding to both attacks on July 22, 2011 (Ergenbright and Hubbard 2012).

During the afternoon of July 22, the suspect parked a rented Volkswagen Crafter van at the base of a building near government offices in Oslo. The vehicle, a vehicle-borne improvised explosive device (VBIED), contained a homemade mixture of fertilizer and fuel creating approximately 2,000 pounds of explosive material. The target of the VBIED was the prime minister's office building. Once the suspect parked the vehicle, he ignited a delayed fuse, walked away from the device, and entered a vehicle he had prepositioned to escape the area. The suspect was dressed and disguised as a Norwegian police officer during this time and he quickly fled the area at a high rate of speed (Ergenbright and Hubbard 2012).

At approximately 15:27 hours, the VBIED exploded, severely damaging the prime minister's building along with four other nearby buildings. Damage from the explosion was significant and extended throughout a four- to five-block radius. The bomb blast killed eight people and injured an additional 90. The timing of the attack, which coincided with a significant lull in street and pedestrian traffic due to summer vacation, is believed to have lessened the human toll. In the end, the attack accomplished one of the suspect's primary goals: occupy and distract law enforcement resources while he transitioned to and executed his primary attack on Utoya Island (Ergenbright and Hubbard 2012).

The island of Utoya, Norway is approximately 26 miles northwest of Oslo and located within the Tyriforden Lake. The island is privately owned by the Norwegian Labor Party and is used as a summer camp for children of Labor Party members. According to Ergenbright and Hubbard (2012), the island had been considered one of the "safest places on earth" due to the remote location and peaceful surroundings. The small island, only accessible by boat, contains approximately eight structures including the main building, conference center, school house, bath house, barn, and cafeteria.

After deploying the VBIED and traveling to the ferry landing site for the island of Utoya, the suspect loaded his weapons, additional ammunition, magazines, and tactical supplies into a large duffle bag and attempted to board the ferry. Still dressed as a police officer, the suspect aroused the suspicion of the ferry operator who demanded second identification from the suspect before allowing him to board the ferry. The suspect reported he had been sent to the island to brief the staff and campers about the bombing in Oslo and to ensure everything was secure. Once satisfied with the suspect's

identity and his purpose for visiting the island, the ferry operator assisted the suspect with loading his equipment onto the
ferry and then transported him to the island. Once at the
island ferry landing, the operator again helped the suspect off-
load his equipment, including a mini Ruger .223-caliber rifle
and a Glock 19 9mm pistol, and introduced him to the island
supervisor and an off-duty police officer (Ergenbright and
Hubbard 2012).

The suspect requested the staff to gather all of the children campers in the main building. Although it is believed the
staff and off-duty police officer were skeptical of the suspect's
police uniform and credentials, the children were gathered as
requested. At approximately 16:53 hours, the suspect pulled
out a weapon and immediately gunned down the off-duty
police officer and staff member before turning the weapon on
the children. For the next 1 hour and 2 minutes, the suspect
had complete control over the island of Utoya, randomly walking around murdering 69 children and wounding an additional
60 (Ergenbright and Hubbard 2012).

During the rampage, the suspect hunted the children
throughout the island and buildings, shooting groups of children as they clung to each other. Trying to escape the shooting, many children jumped into the frigid water and attempted
to swim away from the gunman. The suspect used this opportunity to shoot the children in the water. Other students, fleeing down an extremely narrow trail with steep 50- to 100-foot
cliffs along one side, attempted to climb down the cliffs and
hide among the rocks to avoid the suspect. Many children also
played dead in an attempt to avoid being shot or shot again if
they had already been wounded. Some children were killed
this way when the suspect walked by, shooting them in the
heads as they lay motionless on the ground (Ergenbright and
Hubbard 2012).

The initial emergency calls to the police from Utoya created
a great deal of confusion about the ongoing massacre. Many
of the initial 112 calls, equivalent to 911 in the United States,

were made to the local Buskerud emergency dispatch center, which had primary police response jurisdiction for Utoya. The Joint Operations Center (JOC) in Oslo, two districts removed from Buskerud District, also received phone calls regarding the ongoing shooting. Students stranded on the island were calling their parents in Oslo who, in turn, called the police about the ongoing attack. The emergency phone lines in Oslo were overwhelmed with calls about the bombing in the government center, and although the Oslo JOC would ultimately be responsible for an attack of this magnitude, the emergency calls were transferred to the Buskerud emergency dispatch center. Once the scope of the attack was determined at the Oslo JOC, the DELTA team was dispatched from Olso at 17:38 hours (Ergenbright and Hubbard 2012).

In all the confusion between the bombing in Oslo and the ongoing shooting on the island of Utoya, one fortunate break for the first responders occurred when the daughter of the Police Directorate's liaison to DELTA called her father from the island informing him of the attack. Her father, without hesitation, alerted and authorized the DELTA team to stop conducting search and rescue operations at the bombing scene in Oslo and immediately deploy to Utoya Island at 17:30 hours. By the time DELTA received the official dispatch from the Oslo JOC, they had already been driving for 8 minutes toward the island. Unfortunately, the exact location of Utoya Island was in question and the DELTA operators relied on their personal cell phones to retrieve GPS directions, which were later confirmed by the Oslo JOC (Ergenbright and Hubbard 2012).

The response of the DELTA operators would again be hampered by technological deficiencies resulting from differing radio infrastructures between police districts. Again, using improvisation, the responders managed to communicate with Buskerud Police Department and find their way, in the rain and heavy traffic, to the ferry landing leading to Utoya Island. However, more frustrations ensued when upon arrival at the ferry landing, the DELTA operators learned the local police forces had moved the staging point for the ferry more than 2 miles north of the primary landing point. The DELTA team could hear the gunshots coming from the island; however, they had no transportation at the primary ferry landing to transport them to the island. The team again regrouped and quickly traveled to the new ferry landing where they met up with local police forces that had a police boat and were awaiting DELTA's arrival (Ergenbright and Hubbard 2012).

Once DELTA had linked up with the local police officers, they loaded their gear onto the police boat and began traveling across the lake to the island. Approximately halfway across the lake, the motor on the boat stalled when water mixed with the fuel, possibly due to the heavy load of operators and gear. Two civilian boats were then acquired and used to move the DELTA team to the island. These police officers, arriving at 18:26 hours, were the first police officers to arrive on the island, 1 hour and 33 minutes after the shooting began (Ergenbright and Hubbard 2012).

The DELTA operators, arriving in two separate boats, landed and began moving quickly onto the island in search of the shooter. According to Ergenbright and Hubbard (2012), as one team prepared to enter and secure the schoolhouse, one of the team members noticed the "distinctive white and black checkered pattern of the reflective tape worn at the mid-calf level on the legs of all Norwegian police uniforms in a cluster of trees" near the schoolhouse. The DELTA operators then transitioned from the school house toward the trail where the suspect had been observed. While the team moved, the suspect fled down the trail, dropping his rifle, but then turned and walked back toward the DELTA team with his hands in the air to surrender. The suspect was taken into custody at 18:32 hours, ending the worst mass murder in Norwegian history (Ergenbright and Hubbard 2012).

The police response to the Norway shooting on Utoya Island drew great criticism, tough questions, and calls for greater emergency response preparedness. According to

Ergenbright and Hubbard (2012), DELTA "believes that all police responders acted accordingly and as quickly as they could have." Similarly to the situation at Virginia Tech University, where the suspect murdered two students before engaging in the mass shooting at Norris Hall, the bombing of the prime minister's building in downtown Oslo actually "decreased DELTA response time by placing 22 members of the Counter Terrorist unit in full kit and forward deployed to the bomb site. Without this circumstance, the DELTA response to Utoya may have been further delayed" (Ergenbright and Hubbard 2012).

The Mexico Threat

The threat of a small-arms attack on American soil by terrorist organizations doesn't just exist halfway around the globe. A stone's throw across the Rio Grande River, separating Texas from Mexico, Mexican drug trafficking organizations (DTOs) have used the active shooter tactic in their ongoing turf battles for control of lucrative drug trade routes. In a country where the police and military are struggling to provide security and protection against the heavily armed and organized cartels, the active shooter tactic is proving to be an efficient method of creating chaos and panic among the citizenry.

On February 4, 2012, a lone gunman entered a nightclub in Mexico during the early morning hours, shooting and killing nine people and wounding an additional eleven (Gerardo 2012). Occurring in the city of Chihuahua, Mexico, 237 miles south of El Paso, Texas, this should remind all American law enforcement officials that this small-arms, active shooter attack model is being used by terrorist organizations and being successfully deployed very close to home. In addition, there are numerous documented instances of drug cartel violence already occurring in Arizona, Texas, and many other states (McCaffrey and Scales 2011).

The city of Torreon, Mexico, in the state of Coahuila, has been the scene of several violent active shooter attacks in the past few years. Located just 350 miles south of Eagle Pass, Texas, this community has been repeatedly attacked by drug traffickers and dozens of innocent victims have been gunned down. In one attack, which occurred on June 3, 2012 at a church-operated drug rehabilitation center, multiple gunmen walked into the clinic opening fire. The attackers arrived in two pickups using assault rifles and pistols to shoot and kill 11 victims and wound 8 others (Gerardo 2012). The gunmen fled the scene prior to police arrival. This attack came almost a year to the day after a similar attack on a drug rehabilitation center also in Torreon. In that attack, which occurred on June 7, 2011, a group of gunmen arrived in five vehicles and attacked the La Victoria Alcohol and Drug Rehabilitation Center. Eleven victims were killed in this attack and two others were critically wounded (Gerardo 2011, 2012).

In yet another active shooter attack in Torreon, gunmen pulled up to a party hall where a large party was being held, blocked the exits, and started shooting into the crowd. This attack, which occurred on July 18, 2010, killed 17 of the party-goers and was the third such mass shooting attack in 2010 in that city. In January and again in May, local bars were attacked by gunmen killing a total of 18 victims (Malkin 2010).

Ciudad Juarez, Mexico, known as one of the deadliest cities in the world and located directly across the Rio Grande River from El Paso, Texas, has been the scene of several high-profile active shooter events. On October 22, 2010, gunmen stormed two houses where teenagers were having parties, gunning down 13 victims. The attackers, arriving in two vehicles, opened fire on the parties, firing more than 70 rounds and killing victims ranging in age from 9 to 25. During another party shooting, which occurred on October 17, 2010, nine victims were killed by gunmen who attacked a gathering. In yet another active shooter event, 15 teenagers were killed at a house party in January 2010 (Fox News).

The organized drug trafficking organizations in Mexico appear to be capable of using the active shooter tactic at will against innocent victims across the country. There are very few, if any, examples of Mexican law enforcement or military responding to and actually interdicting an ongoing active shooter event. Whereas historically around the world the active shooter attack is carried out by suspects who make no plans to escape, the attacks being conducted in Mexico are mass shootings by criminals who have every intention of escaping prior to law enforcement arrival. In addition, the attacks in Mexico are being carried out by multiple attackers who are heavily armed and have no fear of fighting to the death against law enforcement and military forces. American law enforcement, especially those within our border states including Texas, New Mexico, Arizona, and California, should be paying very close attention to the tactics being used and deployed by terrorists just across the porous Mexican border.

Since the watershed event at Columbine High School in 1999, active shooter training for patrol personnel and other law enforcement officers who would be the first responders has become standard in most police agencies across the nation. Unfortunately, the criminal element and terrorist groups constantly evaluate and test the readiness and response capabilities of law enforcement. To meet the continuing change in tactics used by criminals, law enforcement officers and trainers must constantly evaluate past active shooter events, both domestically and abroad, to ensure that any identified capability gaps are addressed with training, equipment, and tactical strategies before the next tragedy occurs.

The next chapter provides a detailed analysis of all active shooter events that happened in the U.S. from 2000–2010.

References

After action review. November 2009. III Corps and Fort Hood 05 Nov 09, 17 Nov 2009.

Aurora theater shooting: Police and fire department scanner traffic audio archive. *The Denver Post,* http://www.denverpost.com/breakingnews/ci_21119829/aurora-theater-shooting-police-and-fire-department-scanner (retrieved August 30, 2012).

Bustillo, M., S. Banjo, and T. Audi. 2012. Theater rampage jolts nation. *The Wall Street Journal,* July 21, 2012.

Dehncke, M. 2010. Disruption/prevention of a Mumbai-style terrorist attack. Presentation at the Joint NCTC/DHS/DOJ/FBI/LAPD Counterterrorism Awareness Workshop Series Kickoff Conference, Monterey, CA, November 2010.

Duraphe, A. T. 2009. Final report Mumbai terror attack cases, 26th November 2008 http://www.hindu.com/nic/mumbai-terror-attack-final-form.pdf (retrieved August 29, 2012).

Ergenbright, C., and S. Hubbard. 2012. Defeating the active shooter: Applying facility upgrades in order to mitigate the effects of active shooters in high occupancy facilities. Naval postgraduate school thesis, Monterey, CA, June 2012.

Fox News. Mexico: 13 dead in massacre at Ciudad Juarez party. October 23, 2010. http://www.foxnews.com/world/2010/10/23/mexico-dead-massacre-ciudad-juarez-party/, (accessed September 6, 2012).

Garrett, R. 2012. Lessons learned from Aurora. *Police Magazine,* August 2012.

Gerardo. 2011. Torreon: 11 Youths executed in drug rehab center. *Borderland Beat,* June 8, 2011 http://www.borderland-beat.com/2011/06/torreon-11-youths-executed-in-drug.html (retrieved September 5, 2012).

———. 2012. Nine dead in Chihuahua night club shooting. *Borderland Beat,* February 4, 2012. http://www.borderland-beat.com/2012/02/nine-dead-in-chihuahua-night-club.html (retrieved August 29, 2012).

Giduck, J. 2005. *Terror at Beslan: A Russian tragedy with lessons for America's schools.* Bailey, CO: Archangel Group Inc.

Giduck, J., and W. Chi. 2008. After action review: An evaluation and assessment of the law enforcement tactical response to the Virginia Tech University shootings of Monday, 16 April 2007. Bailey, CO: Archangel Group.

Gunmen kill 11 in Torreon drug rehabilitation center. 2012. *Borderland Beat,* June 4, 2012 http://www.borderlandbeat.com/2012/06/gunmen-kill-11-at-torreon-drug.html (reporter "Ovemex"); (retrieved September 6, 2012).

Harris, B., J. Richman, K. Bender, A. Woodall, and M. Artz. 2012. Former student opens fire at Oakland university, killing 7, April 3, 2012, Mercurynews.com, http://www.mercurynews.com/top-stories/ci_20308252/police-respond-shooting-east-oakland (retrieved September 11, 2012).

Kelly, R. W. 2011. Active shooter recommendations and analysis for risk mitigation. New York City Police Commissioner.

Malkin, E. 2010. Police seek motive in Mexican attack that killed 17. *The New York Times,* July 19, 2010, http://www.nytimes.com/2010/07/20/world/americas/20mexico.html (retrieved September 6, 2012).

Martinez, R. 2005. *They call me Ranger Ray.* New Braunfels, TX: Rio Bravo Publishing.

McCaffrey, B., and R. Scales. 2011. Texas border security: A strategic military assessment. Colgen, LP.

McPartland, R. 2011. Mumbai matters. Presentation at Advanced Law Enforcement Rapid Response Training Center Conference, San Marcos, TX, November 2011.

Nye, S. 2008. NYPD shield: Lashkar-e-Tayyiba (LeT) and the Mumbai operation. NYPD Counterterrorism Bureau.

Patton, P. 2008. NYPD Shield: Tactical analysis of attacks. NYPD Counterterrorism Bureau.

Protecting the force: Lessons from Fort Hood. 2010. Report of the DoD Independent Review.

Remsberg, C. 2006. Mass slaughter in our schools: The terrorists' chilling plan? http://www.killology.com/art_mass_slaughter.htm (retrieved August 28, 2012).

Report of the Virginia Tech Review Panel. 2007. Mass shootings at Virginia Tech, April 16, 2007. Presented to Governor Timothy Kaine.

Virginia Tech University website. 2012. www.vt.edu (retrieved August 10, 2012).

Wollan, M., and N. Onishi. 2012. Gunman kills 7 in a rampage at a Northern California university, April 2, 2012, *The New York Times,* http://www.nytimes.com/2012/04/03/us/fatal-shootings-at-oikos-university-in-oakland-calif.html (retrieved September 11, 2012).

Chapter 3

Active Shooter Events in the United States from 2000 to 2010

With M. Hunter Martaindale

Introduction

The previous chapters provided information on some of the best known or major active shooter events. In this chapter, we focus on providing as complete a picture as possible of all active shooter events in the United States over a 10-year period.

While substantial media and public attention has been focused on active shooter events, relatively little research has attempted to examine collections of these events systematically. To date, only one report has attempted to collect all active shooter events (NYPD 2011). While this report is useful and the most comprehensive collection of active shooter events (ASEs) completed to date, the analysis presented is limited and focused on recommendations for businesses rather than law enforcement agencies. Additionally, the analysis is based solely upon media accounts. Other ASE collections exist, but these tend to be focused on a single type of active shooter event, such as school shootings, and suffer from the same limitations as the NYPD report (see, for example, Lieberman 2008).

Methodology

Search Strategy

Lexis-Nexis was utilized to search for news stories from 2000 to 2010 detailing active shooter events in the United States using the following search terms: active shooter, mass shooting, shooting spree, spree shooting, business shooting, mall shooting, and school shooting. Possible active shooter events were identified from these searches and then evaluated to see if they met the following definition of an active shooter event: An active shooter event involves one or more persons engaged in killing or attempting to kill multiple people in an area occupied by multiple unrelated individuals. At least one of the victims must be unrelated to the shooter. The primary motive appears to be mass murder; that is, the shooting is not a by-product of an attempt to commit another crime. While many gang-related shootings could fall within this category, gang-related shootings were excluded from this study because they are not considered to be active shooter events by the police (NYPD 2011). Two coders examined each candidate event to see if it met the requirement of this definition. In no case did they disagree on whether or not a case should be included or excluded (For a complete list of events, see Appendix A.).

In order to check the completeness of our list, we checked the events that we had identified against other lists/collections of active shooter events. For example, it is common in the wake of an active shooter event for newspapers to publish lists of similar events. We also compared our list of events to the list of shootings published in the NYPD (2011) report and other existing collections (for example, Lieberman 2008; Smith and Supiano 2008). In no instance did we find a case in one of these other sources that we had not identified through our search process. While it is always possible that we missed a case, we believe that the collection of events presented here is close to the complete population of events that occurred in the United States in the last decade.

Data

In order to analyze the events, we first had to gather accurate data. The data presented here come from three sources: reports from the investigating agencies, the supplemental homicide reports (SHRs) produced by the FBI, and news stories. We considered the investigating agency reports to be the most valid data, followed by the SHRs; news reports were considered the least reliable. If the data that we sought to code were reported in the agency reports, we used them. If the agency reports did not contain the data, we sought them in the SHRs; finally, if the data were not available elsewhere, we obtained them from the news reports. When we were forced to use news reports, we used the most recent story that we could find. We believe that this improved the reliability of the information because this gave the story more time to mature and the reporter more time to gather accurate information. Overall, when a particular piece of data was available from all three sources, the reliability between the sources was quite high.

Agency reports were obtained through freedom of information requests. Out of the 84 events in the last decade that we identified, 42 (50%) agencies supplied us with the requested information. We were able to locate data on 46 of the 84 (55%) events in the SHRs. If the event did not include a homicide, it was not listed in the SHRs. Also, Florida is absent from all the SHRs, and some events (19–23%) we were simply unable to locate. As mentioned previously, we used news stories to identify the events, so we had news reports on all 84 events.

Coding

Next, we turned to coding the information so that it could be analyzed. Two coders assessed the variables and their agreement with each other was analyzed to assess reliability. The agreement on the variables ranged from 77% to 100%. This is well above the 70% that is generally considered acceptable in social science.

Results

In this section, we present the results of our analysis. We begin with some basic information on the frequency and characteristics of the events. Next, we provide information about the shooter. Following that, we present information on how the events were resolved.

Characteristics of the Events

Frequency

Figure 3.1 shows the number of active shooter events by year. As can be seen, we identified substantially more events in 2009 and 2010 than in the previous years. This might be an artifact of our search strategy in that the archiving or searchability of news stories may have improved in more recent years, or it could indicate an upward trend in the number of these events. Our informal tracking suggests that 2011 and 2012 also had higher levels of ASEs than we discovered before 2009.

Locations

Figure 3.2 shows the primary attack locations of the ASEs that we identified. Schools were the most frequently attacked type of location, but if business-related location types (factory/warehouse, office, and retail) are combined, businesses were

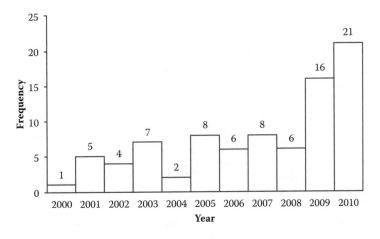

Figure 3.1   Frequency of ASE by year.

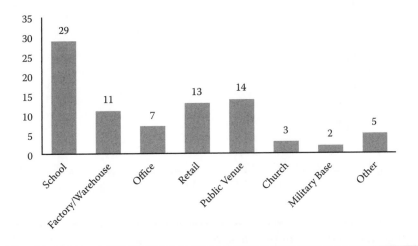

Figure 3.2   Attack location type.

attacked more often than schools. Figure 3.3 shows that 80% of the ASEs occurred at a single location and that, in 20% of the events, multiple locations were attacked.

Number Shot and Killed

The number of people shot in each of the events is presented in Figure 3.4. The number of people wounded in the events

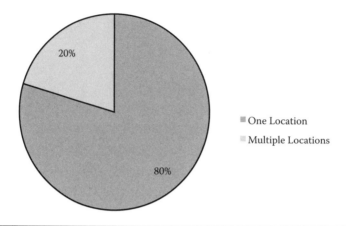

Figure 3.3   Number of attack locations.

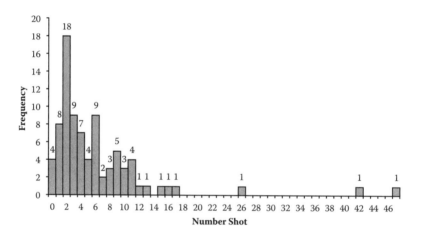

Figure 3.4   Number of people shot.

ranges from a low of 0 to a high of 48. Because the distribution of the data is not normal, the median (or middle value) is probably the best measure to summarize the average number shot. The median number of people shot was four. Figure 3.5 depicts the number of people killed in each attack. The number of deaths ranged from 0 to 32. The median number of deaths was two.

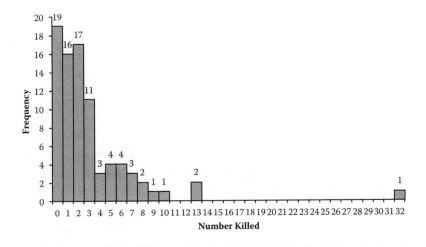

Figure 3.5   Number killed.

Police Response Time

The length of time that passed from the initial active shooter report to law enforcement (generally a 911 call) until law enforcement arrived is presented in Figure 3.6. The median law enforcement response time was 3 minutes. The length of time from the initial report until the active shooter was apprehended displayed a great deal of variance. These times are offered in Figure 3.7. The median time from first report

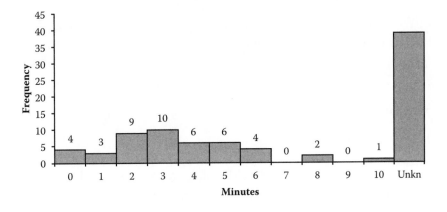

Figure 3.6   Police response time.

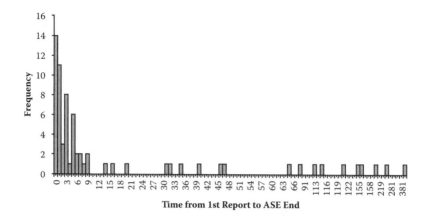

Figure 3.7   Time from first report until the shooter was stopped.

until the ASE ended was 3 minutes. The vast majority (73%) of shooters were stopped within 9 minutes. In those cases where the shooter was at large longer, a change in the situation from an active shooter to a hostage/barricade scenario was the most common. In these events, the shooting had stopped even though the event was technically still ongoing. For instance, in the longest event, law enforcement arrived on scene 4 minutes after being notified. A SWAT team performed entry 18 minutes later. The shooter was barricaded for approximately 7 hours until a SWAT team ended the event. These barricaded shooter events accounted for four of the eight furthest outliers. The other four consisted of two mobile shooters and two who fled the initial attack location and were apprehended some time later.

The Shooter

Demographics

As can be seen if Figure 3.8, shooters were overwhelmingly, but not exclusively, male. Figure 3.9 depicts the ages of the shooters. The youngest was 13 and the oldest was 88; most of the shooters were between 21 and 50.

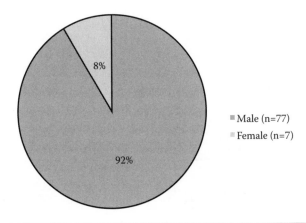

Figure 3.8 Shooter sex.

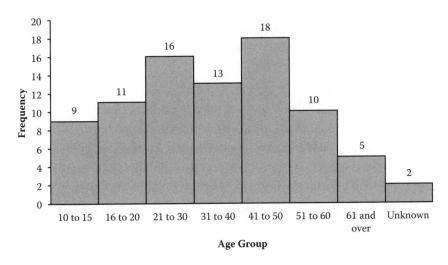

Figure 3.9 Shooter age.

Shooter Relationship with Victim

As evidenced in Figure 3.10, 33 (39%) of ASEs involved shooters who did not have any apparent relationship to the shooting location(s). In 23 cases, the shooter was an employee or former employee. The shooter was a student or former student in 19 of the cases. In three cases, the shooter was a member of the church that was attacked. The relationship of the shooter

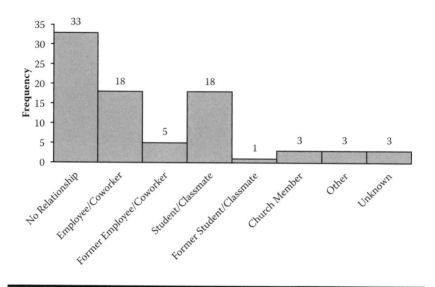

Figure 3.10   Shooter–victim relationship.

to the attack location was classified as "other" in three cases, and the relationship of the shooter to the attack location was unknown in three cases. The three locations that were classified as "other" included a maintenance yard for a bus transit company where the shooter was not affiliated, a nursing home, and a mobile shooter who shot a man on a street corner and then drove to a business that he was not an employee of to continue shooting.

Extensive Preparation

While all of the shooters engaged in at least some planning, some of the shooters engaged in substantially more preparation than others. We coded a case as involving extensive preparation if there was evidence that the shooter engaged in planning beyond acquiring the weapons and ammunition needed to conduct the attack. Evidence of extensive preparation included obtaining or drawing diagrams of the attack location, possessing a "hit list," wearing body armor, or acquiring the equipment/supplies needed to trap victims in the

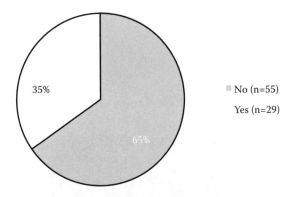

Figure 3.11   Evidence of extensive preparation.

location or slow law enforcement response (such as chains for the door). Preparing a manifesto, blogging about the attack, or developing a media kit was also taken as evidence of extensive planning. Figure 3.11 shows that extensive planning was not involved in 65% of the ASEs. The remaining 29 (35%) events involved extensive planning.

Weaponry

As Figure 3.12 shows, a pistol was the most powerful weapon used in the majority (50–60%) of the events. Rifles were the next most popular weapon and were used in 27% of the attacks. Figure 3.13 shows that most shooters (57%) were armed with a single weapon. Shooters rarely (three cases) wore body armor (see Figure 3.14). The shooter also had explosives in two attacks (see Figure 3.15).

Resolution of Event

The active shooter events in our study were resolved (defined as the shooter being shot, subdued or stopped through direct force other than being shot, or stopping shooting and leaving the location) before law enforcement arrived almost half the time (see Figure 3.16).

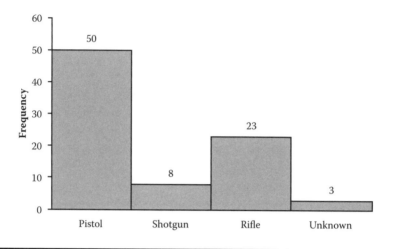

Figure 3.12 Most powerful weapon used.

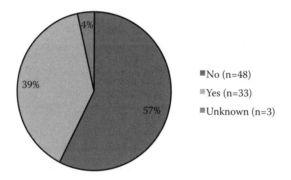

Figure 3.13 Presence of multiple weapons.

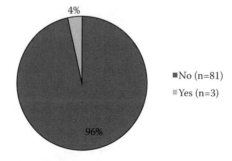

Figure 3.14 Presence of body armor.

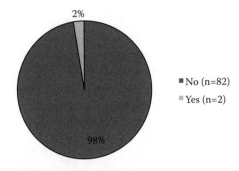

Figure 3.15 Presence of explosive devices.

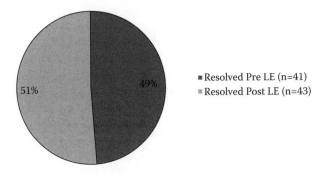

Figure 3.16 ASE resolved before or after law enforcement arrival.

Figure 3.17 provides a more specific depiction of how the shooter was stopped. In 25 of the cases, the attacker simply stopped the attack before the police arrived. In four of these cases, the attacker left the scene. In the other 21, the attacker committed suicide.

In 16 cases, the victims of the attack stopped the attacker. In 13 cases, the victims physically subdued the attacker. In three of the cases, the victims shot the attacker with their personal firearms. One of these cases involved an off-duty law enforcement officer. The other two involved regular citizens.

The attacker was stopped after the police arrived in 43 cases. In 21 of these cases, the attacker stopped himself either

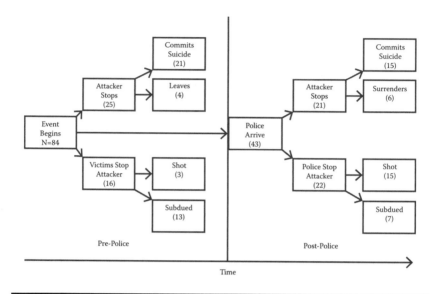

Figure 3.17 Resolution of active shooter events in the United States (2000–2010).

by committing suicide (15 cases) or surrendering to the police (6 cases).

The police used force to stop the attacker in 22 cases. In the majority of these cases (15), the police shot the attacker. In the rest (7), they physically subdued the attacker.

Discussion

This chapter provided detailed information on ASEs that occurred in the United States from 2000 to 2010. Our search identified 84 active shooter events. The typical event occurred either in a business location (factory/warehouse, office, or retail store) or a school and only one shooter was present. The shooter also stayed in the same location. An average of two people were killed and a total of four were shot. It took the police an average of 3 minutes to arrive on the scene after receiving the first notification of the shooting. In about half of the events, the shooting had stopped by the time that the police had arrived. The most common reason for this stoppage was that the shooter had already killed himself at the time of police arrival.

In the events where the shooting was still ongoing at the time of police arrival, the shooter was stopped, on average, in 4 minutes after the police arrived. In these cases, it was equally likely that the shooter would kill himself or be shot by the police.

The typical shooter was between the ages of 21 and 50 and male. Most commonly, the shooter was armed with a single weapon and this weapon was a pistol. While the shooter often had some connection to the attack location (such as being a student at the school or an employee of the business), it was also common for the shooter to have no apparent connection to the attack location.

For the rest of the book, we will refer to this typical ASE as a "basic complexity active shooter event." Approximately 35 of the 84 (42%) events that we identified fell into this category. The knowledge, skills, and abilities (KSAs) needed to deal with this type of attack form the bare minimum that active shooter training should address.

Our analysis, however, clearly shows that not all ASEs fit into the basic complexity category. We refer to attacks that require additional KSAs as "moderate complexity ASEs." Attacks that included multiple shooters, mobile or outdoor shooters, explosives, gas, attempts to barricade entrances, and shooters with body armor or long arms (rifles, carbines, and shotguns) fall into this category because they require capabilities that exceed those needed to deal with basic complexity ASEs. More than half (49 of the 84, 58%) of the events that we identified contained at least one of these complexities, making it more difficult to deal with than the basic complexity ASE. Most of these events contained only a single added complexity. Because these complexities are fairly common, we will argue for the rest of the book that active shooter training should also address these issues if law enforcement agencies want their people to be prepared adequately.

We will refer to the final category of ASEs as "high complexity." These events involve multiple teams of trained attackers simultaneously attacking multiple locations. In other words, these are coordinated terrorist attacks. The Mumbai attack discussed in Chapter 2 is a good example of this type of attack. Fortunately, we have not witnessed any of these attacks on US soil; however, these attacks have occurred in other countries, and there is some suggestion that this type of attack is becoming favored by terrorists. It is therefore important to give some thought to this type of attack. This is done in the following sections of the book.

References

Lieberman, J. A. 2008. *School shootings: What every parent and educator needs to know to protect our children.* New York: Kensington.

NYPD (New York Police Department). 2011. Active shooter: Recommendations and analysis for risk mitigation. New York: New York Police Department.

Smith, L., and B. Supiano. 2008, February 15. Major shootings on American college campuses. *Chronicle of Higher Education.*

Chapter 4

Preparing for the Event

Introduction

The paradigm shift that occurred throughout American law enforcement agencies after the Columbine shootings caused a resurgence in tactical training for first responders. Many agencies had reserved tactical training for only those officers whose assignments required them to be well versed in working tactically as a team. After all, police doctrine before Columbine required that if an emergency tactical situation occurred, first responders would contain the incident and call for specialized units trained and equipped to deal with the event. Many agencies continued to train officers in officer safety issues like firearms and traffic stops, but most officers received limited to no tactical training as it related to working as a member of a team.

The outcry from American citizens who witnessed the events of the Columbine massacre unfold on their television screens was a shock to many in the law enforcement community. In the days following the tragedy, talk radio and television news captured the raw emotional response of many American citizens to what they had witnessed. Many were shocked to see uniformed officers crouched down behind their cars, weapons in hand but apparently frozen and doing nothing to intervene on behalf of the innocent children trapped inside. "I would rather see dead cops than dead kids" seemed to be the common theme.

Those of us in law enforcement at the time understood why the officers were not making entry; those first responding officers were not empowered to. Policy forbade it and not just in Jefferson County Colorado. This was the industry standard at the time: Contain and hold for specialized teams to enter and solve the problem. It was only after the emotions on both sides calmed and logic prevailed that law enforcement agreed to some extent that the outcry of the citizens had merit. No rational person wants to see dead cops or dead children, but it is the duty of law enforcement to protect those who cannot or will not protect themselves. In making this realization, there was only one thing that could address the problem of public mass murder: Empower, equip, and train those first responding officers on scene to execute an immediate rapid response.

There is no doubt that many of the first responders at the Columbine massacre struggled individually with the prospect of violating department policy and rushing inside. After all, some of the first responders' children were inside that school. Their first reaction was to get inside the building and to hunt those responsible for the murder of innocent children. It was not the fear of death that prevented many from rushing in; rather, it was the fear of violating policy, fear of doing something that others would say was wrong, and/or the fear of losing their careers that kept many at bay and no doubt feeling helpless. With this in mind, we lay out the two primary goals of active shooter response.

Primary Goals of the Active Shooter Response

Stop the Killing

As law enforcement administrators struggled to find answers and implement a radically different response protocol, others worried about empowering the first responding officers with the authority to act immediately in defense of innocent people being murdered. Some argued that training first responders in basic tactical skills would cause officers to think that they were now certified SWAT team operators. Many feared that first responders, with their newfound skills and authority to act, would now be more apt to rush into situations that truly require a traditional tactical response by a well equipped and trained tactical team. No matter how you felt about training first responding officers, almost all agreed that something had to be done, and the old ways were no longer an acceptable option. Everyone agreed that it was a law enforcement officer's job to STOP THE KILLING of innocent persons.

To STOP THE KILLING is the number one goal of most active shooter training courses. Depending on the totality of the circumstances surrounding the event, this simple directive can be done in a variety of ways. Unfortunately, the shooter will more than likely dictate what must be done to stop the killing. These responses will normally be to neutralize, isolate, or distract the offender. Each of these is discussed next.

Neutralize the Offender

In many cases, attackers will neutralize themselves either before or just after the police arrive. Most active shooter situations occur in locations where the shooter has access to a large number of potential victims in a small or confined area. These cowards normally choose locations where they feel quite certain that their victims either will not fight back or will be incapable of fighting back once the murderous rampage begins. Most realize that once they expose their intentions, the time before armed officers confront the attacker will be limited. As we saw in Chapter 3, many will kill themselves before or at the first sign of police response. This is not the response of someone who is seeking a fight. It is a coward's exit from the ultimate in cowardly acts. In cases where active shooting is ongoing upon the arrival of the officers, the officers will enter the building, seek out the shooter, and neutralize the shooter using the appropriate level of force (usually gunfire).

Isolate the Offender

In cases where the shooter has not been neutralized, the killing can also be stopped by isolating the shooter from potential victims. In some cases, the shooter will isolate himself or herself and create a barricade situation. In situations where the shooter stops shooting and self-isolates inside a small area with limited access to the rest of the building, officers should follow standard protocols for a barricade/hostage situation. Once the shooter is barricaded and not actively killing, it is a situation best resolved by a specialized tactical unit if available. In this type of situation, first responders should not relax too soon. They should continue to make sure and complete the five Cs:

1. Contain the shooter.
2. Control ingress and egress points.
3. Communicate with shooter, victims, other team members, responding elements, etc.
4. Call for specialized units (tactical and negotiations).
5. Create an immediate action plan in case the shooter should decide not to wait for a tactical unit to arrive to resolve the situation. This plan should address what to do if the shooter
   a. Surrenders
   b. Releases hostages
   c. Makes demands
   d. Begins to execute hostages

In cases where the shooter does not isolate himself or herself, officers can also begin to isolate the shooter from potential victims by entering the building. As the officers move through the building, they are taking control of the areas that they move through and preventing the shooter from moving freely to new areas. This can limit the number of victims to whom the shooter has access.

Distract the Offender

The mere arrival of officers on the scene may distract the shooter and cause him or her to stop murdering the innocent as the shooter maneuvers to evade or confront officers. The mere presence of first responding officers can change the shooter's actions from offensive to defensive. This defensive action may create a hostage barricade situation that will again be dealt with as a traditional tactical response. Regardless of the specific technique(s) used to stop the killing, once the killing is stopped, the second goal of active shooter response must be addressed.

Stop the Dying

The second goal of responding to an active shooter scene is to STOP THE DYING. Once the shooter has been stopped, there will likely be victims that require medical attention. For some victims, this medical attention will need to be immediate if they are to survive. In most cases, emergency medical personnel will not be on scene or will not be allowed to enter because the scene has not been secured by law enforcement. It is quite common during active shooter attacks for the police to receive many, often conflicting descriptions of the shooter(s). This means that even when the police find the dead body of a shooter, they cannot be certain that this was the only shooter. The police must therefore search the entire facility for other shooters before they can declare it clear.

In a facility such as a school, mall, or factory, this search can take hours. This means that it will be hours until emergency medical services (EMS) will enter the attack site. Knowing this reality, it is important that first responding officers have some life-saving capabilities. Training and simple medical adjuncts such as commercial tourniquets, gauze, and bandages can go a long way in saving the lives of victims injured and trapped inside the crisis site. Remember that if emergency medical personnel are not immediately able to access the scene, it will be up to the first responding officers to stop the dying.

As of right now, medical training for first responding officers is limited. The best model of effective response to the types of injures that are likely to be present on an active shooter scene comes from the military. Though many would argue that there is a huge difference between soldiers engaged on the battlefield in another country and a mass shooting inside the United States, many of the wounds will be quite similar. Penetrating trauma caused by gunfire and explosions are the wounds most likely to be faced in either venue regardless of location. Tactical Combat Casualty Care (TCCC), the medical response protocol currently taught to all service members, has saved the lives of countless members of our armed forces over the past decade of conflict. This training is basic and will give those who do not work in a medical specialty the skills needed to intervene and provide immediate life-saving intervention prior to medically trained professionals entering into the scene.

The Committee for Tactical Emergency Casualty Care (CoTECC) was formed to help transition the lessons learned on the battlefield to civilian high-threat medicine. The committee includes physicians, paramedics, emergency medical technicians (EMTs), law enforcement officers, and firefighters—all with an equal vote. By using the model set forth by TCCC in the military arena, TECC hopes to take the lessons learned on the battlefield and transfer them to civilian crisis response in order to reduce deaths in both first responders and the civilian population. This training is much needed and will no doubt help to stop the dying once the killing has been stopped. TCCC and TECC will be discussed in more detail in Chapter

7. With these goals in mind, we turn to discussing the preparation that is needed to accomplish the goals. This includes concept and principle-based training, the proper mind-set, and equipment.

Concept and Principle-Based Training

General Training Philosophy

It is imperative that those called upon to stand the line between the innocent and predators are prepared both mentally and physically for the challenges they will face. Advanced Law Enforcement Rapid Response Training (ALERRT) promotes *concept and principle*-based training. The tactics build from what most first responders learned in their initial professional training and give officers flexibility to adapt the tactics and techniques to fit the specific needs of the situation. It is important to remember that many of the concepts of this training are not inherently natural and may prove challenging for some.

Every first responder will bring strengths and weaknesses into the training environment. Most students in a course will suppress their egos if the issue of ego is addressed properly as a group at the beginning of training. However, for some this is impossible. As an instructor, it is important not to focus too much time or energy on these students. Instructors must stay on track and focus on those students secure enough in their abilities to put their egos away and attempt what they have asked them to do.

The goal of training must be to give the first responder basic tactics and techniques that will increase his or her ability to respond effectively and save innocent lives. Instructors must always remember that the first responders they train may save the life of someone they love! It is this passion and focus that should drive you, as an instructor; after all, the lives saved will be those loved by someone.

Instructors must be the example. Participants emulate what they see, so be professional and passionate about your subject matter. It is important that you know the material and can explain it as well as demonstrate it.

It is easy to get frustrated with some participants who are having problems attempting to use the new techniques, especially under stress. Though the techniques themselves are not new, the application of the techniques to responding to an active shooter may be. It is important to reflect on your own performance when you were first introduced to the tactics and techniques.

Humility is probably the most common characteristic of any great instructor. If the instructor is arrogant and egotistical, he or she will not be effective, and participants will not want to listen to what the instructor has to say, much less learn what he or she is trying to teach them. ALERRT embraces the idea that instructors should always be participants even in their role as instructor. Instructors that normally carry around their ego should leave it at home or in their wall locker when they go to training. If this is you, the best thing to do is permanently deflate your ego and bury it in the back yard before you get yourself or someone close to you hurt or killed.

The skills introduced during training are not overly complex or beyond the ability of most officers to master in their own time. The instructor must try to ensure that the material is not delivered in such a way that it insults officers who have already mastered specific skills prior to attending the course. At the same time, the instructor must deliver the material to the less trained or experienced officers without making them feel the skill is unattainable and therefore nothing but a waste of time to attempt to master.

The need to assess what you can from where you are prior to closing distance on it is an age-old one. The need to shoot the lethal threat surgically and not inflict harm to unarmed people is essential. In the beginning of learning any new tactic or technique, everyone is slower than he or she would like to be. Continued training and mental preparation will assist officers in being able to read a situation and then formulate and initiate a response. This is why repetitive training cycles are created to push students from the unconscious incompetent stage (you do not know what you do not know) through the conscious incompetent stage (you now know what you did not know and can begin working to fix it) to the conscious competent stage (you have to think about it a lot and it is not pretty, but you can do it). Ideally, the unconscious competent stage is what is desired. (You do not have to think about it; you can react instinctively and correctly to the stimulus provided.) That is what people call "advanced." Advanced is nothing more than mastering the basics and being able to do them correctly and very quickly, with little to no warning at all.

ALERRT training strives to take officers through every possible step in the process to respond efficiently and stop the killing during an active shooter event. Students are given the why and how, and it is up to them to determine how they will move through the process on their own. Knowing not just what to do, but also why, is key. Many steps are likely to be missed or maybe not needed at all as the real event unfolds. It is always easier for an officer to know when or where to cheat or deviate from the "system" when he or she *knows* the "system." With no knowledge of a "system" at all, officers will have difficulty solving dynamic problems that require a dynamic response.

Concept and Principle-Based Training

Active shooter response focuses on inserting an ad hoc team into a hostile environment, with limited actionable intelligence to direct the team to the location of the shooter(s). The individual or team must move past uncleared areas as quickly as practicable in order to stop the killing, while simultaneously providing security from counterattack. This counterattack can occur from any angle at any time. We do not assume that the team members even know each other, much less that they have trained together. We also assume that the individual team members have had very limited tactical training. The situation and our assumptions put substantial constraints on what we teach students and how we teach it. We have therefore adopted a concept- and principle-based approach.

Concept and principle-based training is derived from the idea that giving students hard-and-fast rules that must be followed can lead to confusion if or when the tactic does not fit perfectly into the situation or when officers from different training backgrounds are forced to work together during or an actual event. Often the argument over which tactic is better tends to dominate the conversation instead of assessing how successful officers were in achieving a specific operational goal. Responders will spend hours and get seriously angry with each other while arguing one tactic over another—when each tactic may work just fine if applied correctly. Often, one tactic may not be as suitable for some circumstances as another, but responders are often shown tactics in a way that suggests that one tactic is THE way to do it.

Concept and principle-based training relaxes these rules to give students more flexibility to make decisions based upon the totality of the circumstances. It teaches officers how to think about what they are facing and then select a tactic to address that particular problem or issue. A menu of tactics may be learned and practiced, but an understanding of the overall goal is often more important than a preplanned response, which may not achieve that goal or even apply under a certain set of circumstances.

This type of training is more complicated due to the need not only to have to give the students a selection of tactics, but also to teach the students to maintain situational awareness, assess the situation, select an appropriate response, evaluate the effects of the response, and change tactics if needed. Because this is not the easiest way to do business, many in the training world shun this approach. If we are the professionals we purport to be, we need to invest more time, effort, and thought to make ourselves more capable.

The Mind-Set of the Modern First Responder

The goals for first responders to an active shooter scene are pretty clear-cut: (1) stop the killing, and (2) stop the dying. Although this sounds simple enough, an active shooter scene can be one of the most challenging situations faced by law enforcement today. This is especially true if the attack is part of a coordinated terrorist event. As was discussed in Chapter 2, the likelihood of a terrorist engaging in this type of attack on American soil has been increasing. Small-arms terrorist attacks are difficult to detect prior to activation, require limited funding to equip and launch, and can be delivered with pinpoint accuracy in multiple locations simultaneously. Foreign countries around the globe use their military as first responders to any act of terrorism. The Posse Comitatus Act leaves the United States in a precarious situation not faced by any other country as it relates to terrorism response.

The Posse Comitatus Act was passed on June 18, 1878, after the end of Reconstruction, with the intention of substantially limiting the powers of the federal government to use the military for law enforcement activities. The act prohibits most members of the federal uniformed services from exercising state law enforcement, police, or peace officer powers that maintain "law and order" on nonfederal property within the United States.

Who will be the first responders to any act of terrorism inside the United States? The same first responders who responded to the terrorist attacks in New York, Washington, DC, and Pennsylvania on September 11, 2001. The local emergency services (police, fire, and EMS) will be on the frontlines today, just as they were then. There is little doubt that local emergency services will be overwhelmed when dealing with a chemical, biological, radiological, or nuclear attack. Many first responders will leave their posts and fall back to ensure the safety of their own family members, as we saw in the aftermath of Hurricane Katrina.

According to some terrorism experts, the terrorist attacks seen in Beslan, Russia, and Mumbai, India, are a more likely scenario here in the United States than a WMD (weapon of mass destruction) attack. The initial actions of the local emergency services, especially law enforcement, will either embolden or discourage terrorists from mass producing these types of attacks across the country. If law enforcement fails to show that they are capable and effective in confronting the terrorists, the terrorists will be emboldened to continue the attacks.

Capability is much more than attending a training course or two and spending billions of dollars in homeland security money on equipment that sits in a closet at the station or in the trunk of a patrol car. All the training and equipment in the world is rendered useless without the proper first responder mind-set. There are many different names for it: survival mind-set, warrior mind-set, winning mind-set, combat mind-set, etc. Regardless of what you are comfortable calling it, it is simply the willingness to take all of your training and equipment and put it into action during treacherous times. First responding officers must condition themselves on three tiers: physically, skillfully, and mentally. This mind-set is not something that is called upon only in times of crisis; it is a way of living. This mind-set must permeate every aspect of the first responder's daily life.

"One Warrior's Creed," written by Steven R. (Randy) Watt, is a great example of how first responders must prepare for the day they will have to respond to the most dangerous call of their careers. Randy was the assistant chief of police in Ogden, Utah, and a colonel in the Utah National

Guard as well as the commanding officer of the 19th Special Forces Group.

One Warrior's Creed

If today is to be THE DAY, so be it.

If you seek to do battle with me this day you will receive the best that I am capable of giving.

It may not be enough, but it will be everything that I have and it will be impressive, for I have constantly prepared myself for this day.

I have trained, drilled and rehearsed my actions so that I might have the best chance of defeating you.

I have kept myself in peak physical condition, schooled myself in the martial skills and have become proficient in the application of combat tactics.

You may defeat me, but you will pay a severe price and will be lucky to escape with your life.

You may kill me, but I am willing to die if necessary.

I do not fear Death; for I have been close enough to it on enough occasions that it no longer concerns me.

But I do fear the loss of my Honor and would rather die fighting than to have it said that I was without Courage.

So I will fight you, no matter how insurmountable it may seem, and to the death if need be, in order that it may never be said of me that I was not a Warrior.

Randy explains the creed and how it came about in an article written for the National Tactical Officers Association's quarterly publication "The Tactical Edge" (Watt 2008):

> Warriors are natural leaders. When times of crisis
> appear, they are naturally sought out and looked to
> by those for whom the situation is overwhelming. As
> a wise leader once told me, "We don't pay you for
> the day-to-day; we pay you for that occasional time
> of crisis when preparation and action are combined
> to form a resolution."
>
> To be constantly prepared, warrior leaders must
> be committed to something far beyond themselves,
> something that clearly both separates and defines
> them, something on an order of magnitude well
> beyond normal lifestyles.

Randy penned the creed during the closing days of his military tour in Iraq as a counterterrorism advisor to Iraqi security forces. Randy states that he was reflecting on those individuals he had known during his time in Special Forces and SWAT—the truly dangerous and deadly men with whom he had shared fear, sweat, and blood, men committed to the cause of liberty, who believed that it was worth everything they had to give, even their lives. These were men and women who exported their capability to faraway places in the world where terror and tyranny reigned, and who, within the confines of the cities and jurisdictions within the greatest nation on earth, the United States of America, utilized their dedication and skill to protect the rights of those unable or unwilling to protect them for themselves. These men and women truly represented the commitment to selfless service and willing sacrifice honed by previous generations of warriors.

He states that he was reflecting on a recent operation in which a good friend perished. His friend left behind a young family and numerous tears were shed in the days following his death. At a memorial ceremony, words had been spoken—words that indicated the special nature of this friend's service. Randy states that this caused him to ask, "Why do we do this? Why do we, the 'rough men' of whom Orwell speaks, voluntarily subject ourselves to the life-long efforts required to be the warriors, to become one of Dave Grossman's 'sheep-dogs'?" As he reflected, Randy began to recognize some underlying values that are consistent among those police and military special operations colleagues with whom he served. The recognition of the constancy of those values resulted in the writing of "One Warrior's Creed" in an attempt to verbalize the values of the warriors of our great democracy.

If today is to be The Day, so be it. We do not know the day or the time when we will be called on and we do not care. By living, not just practicing, the creed, we will be ready no matter when or where. The day, time, or place does not matter. Stephanie Shugart, wife of MSG Randall Shugart, recipient of the Medal of Honor, said that "it takes a real man to live a creed, not just say it."

*If you seek to do battle with me...*We of the creed do not go looking for the fight; those purveying evil must bring it to us. We, the "quiet professionals," have nothing to demonstrate, nothing to show, no need to brag. We quietly go about our lives. We represent, as stated by the wife of one who lives the creed, "the most dangerous nice guy(s) you'll ever meet." But if you bring the battle to us, *you will receive the best that I am capable of giving.* We are committed to fighting you, to defending ourselves and those for whom we feel responsible, and we will give it our best effort no matter what.

It may not be enough, as we recognize that we do not control the tactical environment enough to ensure the out-come...*but it will be everything that I have to give and it will be impressive, for I have constantly prepared myself for this day.* We recognize that the commitment and responsibility we took upon ourselves by oath requires that we put forth daily effort to ensure our skills are at their utmost when called for. *I have trained, drilled, and rehearsed my actions so that I might have the best chance of defeating you.* Never knowing when, where, or how, we accept the standard of being constantly ready. Daily, we sweat, strain, and push ourselves far beyond the boundaries of mere mortals, then smile and prepare to do it again tomorrow. If the call to action never comes, we are okay with that, but we are not okay with the potential for failure due to a lack of preparation.

I have kept myself in peak physical condition, for a warrior not highly fit is less than half a warrior. *I have schooled myself in the martial skills,* for we recognize that to be truly ready means that we must be capable of the complete range of weapons, including firearms, blunt and edged weapons, personal weapons such as hands, elbows, knees, and feet, and the mind, *and have become proficient in the application of combat tactics.* We understand that since we do not know where or when, we must understand the range of variables existing on any terrain and we must have prepared our strategies for fighting there.

You may defeat me. We know that we are mortal, and we have no false illusions or ideas of being invulnerable—*but you will pay a severe price.* We will inflict upon you whatever pain and injury is necessary to assure your defeat, *and you will be lucky to escape with your life.* We will take your life, without remorse, if you force us to do so. We do not enjoy killing, but we recognize that the taking of the life of an evil predator may be necessary in order to ensure the safety of ourselves, our loved ones, our cherished way of life, and our nation.

You may kill me, but I am willing to die if necessary. We recognize that great sacrifices have been necessary in the past in order to maintain the cause of freedom and to ensure a free society, and we honor those who have died in the cause of liberty. We also recognize that warriors must be willing to do so today and in the future, or the sacrifices of those who have paid the ultimate price in the past will become nothing more than a historical anecdote. *I do not fear death, for I have been close enough to it on enough occasions that it no longer concerns me.* We recognize that all who have received the God-given gift of mortality die, that it is nothing to be feared for it will come to us all. We do not get to choose the place or time of our demise, but we revel in the Roman proverb, "It is better to have lived one day as a lion than one hundred years as a sheep." We have been present when death has occurred and some of us have caused it. We have known warriors among us who have perished. We have honored them, paid tribute to the families who raised and supported them, and thanked God for the privilege of knowing them.

But I do fear the loss of my Honor. To live honorably is the root of our zeal, and it provides the fuel for our efforts, which is why the word is capitalized. We, like the great warrior classes of old, recognize that a life without honor is a life wasted. We are committed to the greater things than ourselves *and would rather die fighting than to have it said that I was without Courage.* Courage is the exemplification of all that we hold in great value, of all that we feel is worth the ultimate price. To ever be without Courage is to truly be unarmed, unprepared, and easily overcome. We can never overstate its importance, which is why it is capitalized.

So I will fight you. We strongly commit to that and exemplify it with how we live the creed, *no matter how insurmountable it may seem and to the death if need be.* We care not what the odds are or what the probable outcome may be. What is important is that we are there and ready *in order that it may never be said of me that I was not a Warrior.* To live in the shame of knowing that we capitulated, that we surrendered to fear, that we failed to exemplify the creed, that we have dishonored those before us is a shame and humiliation beyond comprehension. That is the only thing a warrior truly fears.

The Law Enforcement Warrior

It is unfortunate that in many law enforcement circles across America the term "warrior" is considered taboo. The very mention of the word conjures up illusions of lawsuits, public complaints, and Rambo in a patrol uniform. Much of this is due to a lack of understanding about what truly defines a warrior.

The warrior is the officer you want backing you up on a call where you find yourself outnumbered or outgunned. A warrior is someone you want next to you when you are patrolling the streets of Baghdad or the mountains of the Hindu Kush. A warrior is also the person you want stopping to help a family member who has been stranded on the side of the road when a vehicle breaks down.

Warriors keep their heads when everyone around them is losing theirs. A warrior prays for peace but prepares for conflict. The warrior is selfless, putting the mission and those with him or her above his or her own needs. The warrior is a professional, always polite and willing to help with even the most menial of tasks. The warrior is also capable and prepared to defend himself or herself and others in the blink of an eye. A warrior is not violent but will embrace violence when and where necessary to protect the innocent from the predators of society.

In his book, *Leadership and Training for the Fight,* retired Special Forces soldier and law enforcement trainer Paul Howe explains, "We must be able to apply the appropriate degree of force and discrimination...demonstrating a complete business-like attention to detail and if necessary, we must be able to kill with ruthless efficiency."

Training and equipment will only get a first responder so far. Those who hope that they will never be faced with this type of event should be reminded that "hope" paralyzes and is not a strategy. Too often, officers think in terms of "if/then," when they should be thinking in terms of "when/then." "If" implies that it will most likely never happen and therefore leads to unconstructive and destructive mind-sets like denial and hope: "I can't believe this is happening"; "I hope I can make that shot"; "I hope I will do the right thing." These are all unacceptable mind-sets. The first responder mind-set should be built from known capability through realistic personal preparation. "When" makes it a foregone conclusion that he or she will one day be faced with this situation and must therefore prepare for it. When it happens, the mind-set will be, "I am ready; send me." This is not a statement of arrogance; it is a feeling of knowing that one has done everything to prepare for "The Day." Hope and courage will not be enough; we must prepare ourselves physically, skillfully, and mentally to complete our mission successfully: "Stop the killing and stop the dying."

On-Scene Leadership and the Active Shooter Response

Law enforcement response to critical incidents is usually a managed affair. Law enforcement officers regularly receive training in incident management tools like the "incident command system" or ICS. ICS is defined by the US Center for Excellence in Disaster Management and Humanitarian Assistance as a set of personnel, policies, procedures, facilities, and equipment integrated into a common organizational structure designed to improve emergency response operations of all types and complexities. ICS is a subcomponent of the National Incident Management System (NIMS), as released by the US Department of Homeland Security in 2004.

An ICS is based upon a flexible, scalable response organization providing a common framework within which people can work together effectively. These people may be drawn from multiple agencies that do not routinely work together, and ICS is designed to give standard response and operation procedures to reduce the problems and potential for miscommunication on such incidents. ICS has been summarized as a "first-on-scene" structure, where the first responder to a scene has charge of the scene until (1) the incident has been declared resolved, (2) a more qualified responder arrives on scene and receives command, or (3) the incident commander appoints another individual incident commander.

Management tools like the ICS and managers who can use them effectively are a true asset to any critical incident scene. The active shooter scene, however, will also require leadership. Leadership usually comes in one of two forms: formal or informal. A formal leader is a person who not only carries the authority, rank, or position to be in charge, but also has the leadership attributes to task organize and lead officers inside the crisis site. The informal leader is a person who may not have the authority, rank, or position to be in charge, but who steps up and leads other officers inside the crisis site. Many times this is done when those who are in a leadership position fail to act. The worst possible thing an officer on an active shooter scene can do is fail to act. Failure to act will mean certain death and injury to the innocent trapped by the murderer.

Chief Kimberley Crannis of the Blacksburg, Virginia, Police Department was chastised by those who conducted the official after-action report for the Virginia Tech Shooting because she was part of the initial response into Norris Hall. That is leadership and her actions were right. Position or rank does not relieve one of the duty to protect and serve. The difference between management and leadership is that managers do things right and that leaders do the right thing. Chief Crannis could have very easily stepped off the contact team and no one would have ever found fault with it, except maybe her. She could have stood outside Norris Hall and watched as her officers responded to the unknown, but she did not. She saw herself as an officer first and then as the chief. Too often, officers in positions of authority fail to take on the mantle of leadership and lead from the front.

A good leader will never ask a subordinate to do something that he or she is not willing or able to do. The top priority at the time Chief Crannis entered Norris Hall as a member of a contact team was to stop the murdering of the innocent—not to establish the command post. Other officers, who responded after the initial entry was made, were more than capable of establishing the command post and running the incident command system. As Colin Powell puts it, "The commander in the field is always right and the rear echelon is always wrong, unless proven otherwise."

The initial responding officers to most active shooter scenes will most likely not be those in positions of authority beyond the first-line supervisor level. Chances are that those tasked with the initial response to most scenes will not be formal leaders within their organizations. This means that the informal leaders will have to step up and act. The goal of most active shooter training is to give everyone an understanding of what is expected of first responding officers. Lives hang in the balance and there is often no time for a supervisor to get to the scene and formulate a response. Response must be quick and effective to save lives.

Equipment

Part of the eternal discussion about what capabilities a responder needs to have can be broken down into three main categories: mental, physical, and tactical. Tactical also covers equipment. What equipment should officers have as basic issue, and what additional equipment can be added to enhance performance? In addition to the standard equipment issued to an officer (soft body armor and a pistol), officers must now also think of additional equipment like body armor that will protect against rifle fire, a go-bag with extra ammunition and medical supplies, and equipment for breaching.

Most ideas, when presented in a vacuum, make perfect sense. Often though, when added together, they can spell a nightmare. There is no doubt that additional equipment can enhance performance. With the addition of specialized equipment to enhance performance comes the unfortunate offshoot issue—physical capabilities. What physical conditioning will be required to haul all this nice-to-have gear around? The answer to that question must be explored by each of us individually. Every responder must look at the tasks that reasonably need to be performed under these exigent circumstances and assess what physical condition one must be in to achieve these tasks successfully.

There may be trade-offs that need to be made. These often involve assessing what you get versus what you give up to get it. Often responders get so loaded down with nice-to-have equipment that they can no longer sustain operational readiness. Being reduced to just bare essentials is not an ideal situation either, but missions can still be accomplished. If operating with bare-bones equipment is unacceptable, then you may have to ratchet up your exercise routine in order to perform.

Next we discuss some of the critical pieces of equipment that first responders should have if they seek to maximize their ability to stop the killing and then stop the dying.

Patrol Rifles

Perception (or misperception) is still shaping policy and training. It should be obvious that rifles are more accurate weapon systems at a distance than pistols. It is also becoming more widely known that the ballistic performance of the average rifle duty round in incapacitating a hostile threat is much more desirable than that of a pistol round.

"Distance favors the marksman." This is a true statement and is used to accentuate the need for continued, hard training to improve one's skills with a weapon. In addition, better equipment can definitely improve the marksmanship of the marksman as well. When accuracy means putting surgical and effective lethal force on the intended threat, while not bringing harm to others in the immediate area, a rifle is the best way to do this. The distances at which first responders can expect to have to make critical shots will vary. This distance may be farther than that at which the vast majority of first responders train to use their handguns.

Consider the average hallway length in most schools or at our malls. Look at the distances in parking lots that we may need to move across tactically, under fire, while putting directed fire on a lethal threat. It is important to have the right tools in a properly trained person's hands to maximize effectiveness under these conditions.

Another point that is important to consider is the use of body armor by suspects. As was seen in the North Hollywood shootout, body armor kept pistol rounds from being effective in neutralizing those hostile threats. Once rifles were introduced into the equation, the threats were dealt with quickly. With both accuracy and the ability to defeat body armor in favor of the rifle rounds, again it seems hard to believe that our culture would have difficulty with first responders having this capability when we know the suspects already do (Buziecki).

Go-Bags

Extra ammunition and medical supplies are probably the two most important items officers should consider carrying into a critical scene. The extra ammunition should be loaded into magazines for the weapon systems you are using to cut down on the lag time created by having to pull ammunition out of the box and load up a magazine before being ready to fight.

Medical supplies should consist of at least one tourniquet, bandages, gauze, medical shears, and latex gloves. The more tourniquets carried by first responders, the better. More than one appendage of a victim could require intervention, and massive hemorrhages in a leg can require more than one tourniquet to stop the bleeding. Always have at least one backup, more when possible.

There are cheap and easy items to stock your medical kits and there are also more expensive, store-bought items that work better. All can and do work. When working on limited budgets, we suggest you have some of the high-end gear readily available for yourself on a day-to-day basis and then the less expensive stuff in small zip-lock bags as a backup should a mass casualty event happen.

As with any gear or equipment, most medical equipment requires some level of training to ensure it is being used properly. Too often, agencies will purchase equipment and pass it out to their officers without training them how to use it. It is more of a "check the box" purchase so that administrators can tell the public that their officers are prepared. Without training, this is only half true.

Rifle-Grade Body Armor

We have seen what rifle rounds can do to level 3A body armor and to responders' vehicles. Responders will need to invest in better ballistic protection if they feel that the probability of encountering rifle fire is high (which the data presented in Chapter 3 suggest that it is). First-responding officers should seriously consider acquiring a plate-carrying vest with rifle-grade plates inside.

There are several levels of protection, styles, and weights of rifle plates on the market. Some research is necessary to find a good deal on plates that will afford the protection you seek and also be functional. When we say "functional," we mean you can wear them and still accomplish your mission. These plates, because of their extra protection, add weight to the existing 3A ballistic protection being worn. This extra weight translates to more energy being used to accomplish the same tasks. More energy means that a first responder may not last as long during a mission, be able to go as far, or be able to move as quickly.

Load-Bearing Vests

With the suggested extra equipment being discussed, it will become even more difficult to store, access, and carry all this gear when arriving on a scene and determining if it is needed. There are many varieties of vests on the market. Some are load-bearing vests (LBVs) only, which means they aid in carrying equipment and accessing gear when needed but offer no additional ballistic protection.

These vests have a pouch system on the outside of them that could double as a "go-bag" to house the extra equipment the first responder wishes to have with him or her upon entry into a crisis. Gear that would typically be found inside a go-bag can be put into these pouches to make access easier than sifting through a bag full of various pieces of equipment. These vests vary in price, but are usually very affordable and functional. This system is easier to carry on your person than a bag/strap system, which can be cumbersome, shift around, throw your balance off, and be a distraction.

Plate Carriers

Many plate carriers have a pouch system on the outside as well. The pouches can be fixed or some models can allow for positioning the pouches to the owner's preference. Gear that would typically be stored in a go-bag can be put into these pouches just like the LBVs. This option is ideal because it is an easy system that offers extra equipment access and better ballistic protection, and is much easier to wear than a bag/strap system.

Basic Setup of Equipment

With whatever equipment is being carried, make sure to set it up where it can be accessed quickly and efficiently. As the gear starts to pile on, it is common that it starts to cover the usual path traveled to access a firearm or other critical, time-sensitive gear like a tourniquet, radio, etc. These things will need to be accessible immediately. How your gear is set up on your go-bag, vest, or normal duty wear is critical. Practice accessing this gear on a regular basis to create more efficiency and economy of movement.

Summary

Preparing ourselves and our agencies to respond to an active shooter event is much more than just entering the crisis site and confronting the gunman. First responding officers must be given both the tools and training necessary to improve their odds of saving as many lives as possible. Officers must be trained and equipped to make an emergency entry into the crisis site and to close distance with and contact the shooter in order to *stop the killing*. Officers must also be trained and equipped to handle the chaos that will immediately follow. They must perform vital link-up procedures with other responders and provide emergency live-saving intervention to the wounded in order to *stop the dying*.

Agencies that believe they can prepare their officers for these types of events by showing a 4-hour PowerPoint presentation during their in-service training will find themselves sorely lacking should they be unfortunate enough to have to respond to an actual active shooter event. Every aspect of the response and recovery operation should be studied and no bullshit assessments should be made by the leadership of organizations to ensure their officers are both capable and competent to respond. The lives of the innocent are depending on this!

References

Buziecki, S. 2002. Patrol rifles: Arming officers to succeed. North Aurora Police Department, Patrolrifle.com

Howe, P., U.S. Army retired. 2011. *Leadership and training for the fight*. New York: Skyhorse Publishing.

Watt, R., Retired colonel. 2008. One warrior's creed: A philosophy to live by. The tactical edge. *National Tactical Officers Association Quarterly*, Summer 2008.

Chapter 5

En Route and Actions Outside the Building

En Route

Response starts with the call and what is known prior to arrival. Officers may or may not have sufficient initial information to conclude that this event is being perpetrated by one or more well-armed, organized, and motivated murderers. Often, these facts will not be known until officers begin arriving and hear the sounds of overwhelming gunfire. Communication is key in allowing follow-on responders and supervisors to know what resources to call upon and immediate decisions to make. The incident will require a tactical approach even prior to arriving on the scene.

Prior to arriving on the scene, the first responder must think of the location of the crisis, where he or she will be arriving on the scene, how far away he or she should park, what equipment will be needed, and necessary coordination with any other responders who might be arriving at that time as well. Where will responders meet up? Where and how will responders breach into the crisis site?

In most situations, the first officers on the scene will not be there until the attack has been underway for several minutes. Although the police response in the United States is generally very fast (around 3 minutes), there is still the potential for numerous casualties to occur in that short period of time. The initial responders to the scene may be faced with a flood of escaping and wounded victims. First responding officers must prepare themselves for the chaos and confusion that may be unfolding at the scene upon arrival. If there is actionable intelligence driving the officers to the location of the shooter—such as continued gunfire, human intelligence from victims, or intelligence passed via cell phone from victims trapped inside—officers must bypass the wounded and move as quickly as possible to isolate, distract, and neutralize the gunman. There will be no time to treat or assist in the rescue of the victims. Responding officers must stop the killing before they can stop the dying.

Priorities of Work

The top priority of first responding officers to an active shooter scene is to stop the killing. In what follows, we break this process down into discrete steps: gather intelligence, arrive on scene, approach the crisis site, breach into the structure, enter and confront the shooter.

Gather Intelligence

Intelligence collection begins the moment that the active shooter call is received and will continue throughout response. Intelligence will normally be fragmented at best. Information coming from inside the crisis site is normally coming from panicked victims who are hearing gunshots or have just witnessed an act of violence. It is critical that emergency communication operators are trained in getting specific information about the suspect's location out to the first responding officers as quickly and accurately as possible. Suspect descriptions and weapons are not nearly as important as the location of the gunman inside the crisis site. The suspect's location may play a major role in how first responding officers will approach the crisis site.

There are many different things that officers should consider as information is coming out over the radio. Before the initial responders enter the crisis site, officers should refrain from talking on the radio unless communicating critical information about the response such as rally points and approach routes for initial officers. In our reviews of the radio traffic of officers responding to active shooter scenes, we have found that critical information is often delayed because officers are taking up valuable air time with information not critical to the response.

Emergency communication operators and responding officers should also be aware of time lapses in information. Imagine this scenario: A woman driving home sees what appears to be a male subject dressed in black walking across the playground at the local elementary school. The subject is carrying what appears to be a weapon. The woman struggles with exactly what she thinks she has seen and contemplates calling the local police department to report what she has seen. She does not immediately call and continues to drive home. Meanwhile, calls from inside the school start to flood into the emergency communication center with reports of shots fired inside the school cafeteria. Once the woman arrives home, she decides to contact the authorities about what she had witnessed on her drive home. She advises the emergency communication operator that she has just seen a male subject on the playground at the elementary school dressed in black and carrying what appeared to be a weapon. If an accurate time is not established, it is likely that the first responding officers will respond to the wrong place. The opening moments in an active shooter call will be filled with chaos and unintentional misinformation. As a first responder, understand this will be the norm and do not let it bog you down. Once on the scene, use your powers of observation and move to stop the shooter.

Arrival on Scene

It is difficult to control the adrenaline dump that pulses through your body when you get an in-progress call that requires you to get to a scene quickly. The drive and anticipation of what you will find once on scene can cause this rush of excitement and adrenaline to cloud your judgment. First responders should slow their approach and take a quick survey of the area immediately surrounding the crisis site. If first responding officers have been given accurate and timely intelligence about the shooter's location, this can help them to determine the most appropriate entry point into the scene. Either way, a quick survey of the area may prevent first responders from driving into an ambush.

Officers who have prepared themselves for this type of call should have all the equipment they may need positioned where they can access it quickly once they arrive on the scene. Extra ammunition, breaching tools, and medical equipment should be a part of any prepared first responder's go-bag. The key here is that you have to grab it before you start your approach. If you leave vital tools and equipment in your vehicle, they will remain there. Failing to prepare is preparing to fail.

There are two schools of thought about using lights and sirens when responding to the scene. Some believe that if you approach with lights and sirens on, you will cause the shooter to change focus from innocent victims to the responding officers. Depending on the lighting conditions, this could cause the shooter to focus on the vehicles and give the officers the cover of darkness to move into the crisis point without the shooter knowing where entry was made.

The other option is to approach silently. This gives officers the ability to use their personal senses to gain vital intelligence about what is happening on the scene. Officers should be able to hear gunshots and try to pinpoint their location inside the structure. If the shooter is not aware of the officers' presence, this may give the officers time to move into a position where they can confront the shooter before the shooter knows that the officers are even there.

Both techniques have their merit. First responding officers should use the intelligence information they have received prior to arrival and situational awareness to determine the appropriate arrival response.

Outside the Building

The Initial Team

It has been observed that the optimal size of an ad hoc contact team should be four to five officers. Traditionally, ad hoc teams of six or more first responders result in confusion and take on the characteristics of an unorganized mob with officers failing to understand the exact roles required of them. In large groups, safety issues often arise from the sheer number of officers trying to occupy and operate in a small and confined area. This can make the entire team nothing more than a bumbling, fumbling target trapped in the confines of a sometimes narrow hallway. If a jurisdiction has the resources to commit six or seven officers into the scene as the initial responders, it is generally more effective for these officers to respond by breaking into smaller groups of three or four and attempting to enter the building from different locations. This way, if one team does get pinned down by the shooter or shooters, the second team can respond in a flanking movement to suppress or neutralize the shooter(s).

In most jurisdictions, the reality is that the first contact teams to enter the structure and address an active shooter will consist of one, two, or possibly three officers. A single officer entering the active shooter scene must understand the inherent risk assumed in taking this action. Although this should not be the typical response, first responders should be empowered to make the decision based on the information available at the time and the totality of the circumstances. Again, department policy needs to be aligned to coincide with this tactical paradigm shift.

For example, a school resource officer who hears gunshots down the hallway should not be required to seek cover and concealment until a backup unit arrives on scene to assist. The overriding objective once shots have been fired is to stop the murdering as quickly and efficiently as possible. A single officer who arrives on the scene where shots are being fired should first assess the overall situation and quickly determine if he or she thinks that a solo response is feasible.

The ABCs of Cover

Because first responders may begin to take fire outside of the building where the attack is occurring, cover will be discussed here. In most law enforcement training, the term "cover" is used in the abstract. Phrases like "find some cover" are repeated time and again, and many students never really understand the terminology, cover's limitations, or how to find and get to cover effectively. Every year in America, first responders are murdered trying to find cover when faced with an armed adversary at close distances. Using terrain to mask a responder's movement and limit exposure is critical, but should not take priority once contact has been made, especially at close distances. The ABCs of cover concept gives the first responder a tiered approach to reaching and using cover effectively:

Accurate return fire: Fire-first responders should train to engage an adversary first with accurate and lethal fire-power while moving off the "X." Many times this will serve to minimize the need for immediate "cover." If the officer's rounds are truly accurate and find their mark, the suspect's ability to continue to engage the officer should be significantly reduced. This is not to say that officers should not seek cover during or after an engagement, but officers must understand that reducing the need for immediate cover can be done by "hiding behind their bullets." This should be the officer's first step in finding cover.

Body armor: If the first responder has body armor available, he or she should be wearing it. First responders should train to posture themselves during an engagement to maximize the effectiveness of their body armor. Officers should square their bodies to the origin of the incoming rounds to maximize the protection provided by their body armor. When a responder "blades" his or her body toward a threat, he or she expose holes in the armor. One such hole is the space provided for the arms. A bullet traveling through the shoulder can travel unimpeded by body armor into the upper chest of the officer, with fatal consequences.

Cover: "Cover" is anything that will stop the bullet or projectile from passing through and impacting the first responder. This can be difficult to determine and can change depending on the size (caliber) weapon being used. First responders should be aware that most American construction materials will not stop bullets. Most cover will also degrade with each bullet impact. Material that may be effective in stopping one or two pistol bullets may be compromised with the third impact. Once again, the sooner you can stop the source of incoming bullets, the safer it is for everyone involved.

Officers should train to fire their weapons from cover. Officers sometimes get too close to their cover. Many times this creates a situation where the officer cannot effectively deploy his or her weapon to engage the adversary. This can lead to officers being pinned down and/or flanked because they have limited their area of control to nothing more than a few inches of space between them and their perceived safety blanket.

Approaching the Crisis Site

For first responding officers, just approaching the crisis site may be difficult. Consider the worst-case scenario where officers take fire while trying to approach the crisis site. Those who take the time to plan their murderous rampage will often take into account the inevitable response by law enforcement and establish some type of security element to engage, or, at a minimum, alert the attacker to the arrival of first responding officers. These security elements can wreak havoc on first responding officers as they arrive, thus giving the murderers more time to inflict casualties upon the innocent trapped inside.

Officers should be familiar with different movement techniques designed to be used outside. Unlike being forced down a corridor inside a building, techniques used to cover exterior terrain differ considerably. For instance, you do not want to group up and move over open terrain. This will make you an easy target for anyone prepared for the arrival of first responders.

Leaders should make sure that officers are trained using military small unit tactics like the "wedge" and "bounding overwatch." These techniques will give the officers an understanding of how tactics must be adapted to the changes in environment and terrain. These techniques can be trained starting with dry fire, move to force on force, and culminate, if practical, with live fire exercises.

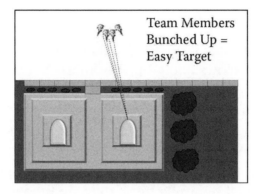

The military has developed, incorporated, and used effectively certain tactics designed to contend with the necessity to close distance with and engage threats over open terrain. These techniques have worked over decades of conflict in various types of terrain.

Officers should be given instruction on proper use of cover and concealment, the use of masking terrain, and actions on contact. Simple techniques, when applied to the approach of the crisis site, can make the difference between an effective response or officers penned down, wounded, and ineffective. As a leader, you must not only prepare yourself and those around you, but also be able to articulate and educate the public why certain tactics are necessary for law enforcement officers to learn. Two specific movement techniques are discussed next.

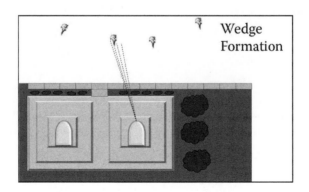

Bounding Overwatch

Bounding overwatch is a coordinated cover and maneuver technique that allows one group of officers to cover for threats while remaining stationary to maximize situational awareness and firing accuracy, while another responder group moves as quickly as they can from one point of cover to another in the direction of the crisis site. When moving, the officers are moving as quickly as they can; therefore, the moving group will not be capable of returning fire if they are fired upon. The covering group is responsible for applying surgically accurate firepower to any threat that appears while the other group is moving.

"Directed fire" is a tactic that should be utilized by the covering officers if a threat begins firing on them from a position where officers cannot get a clear, surgical shot on the suspect. This tactic is sighted fire, which has a slower cadence than what is typically referred to by the military as "suppressive fire." This sighted, slower rate of fire allows for more surgical shots on a threat location and minimizes the effect of gunfire on areas outside the threat's location. This slower rate of fire also serves to conserve ammunition, which may be in short supply depending on the amount of ammunition carried by responding officers. Not knowing how long a particular fight will last and what will be required to end the fight, officers will need to use what they have as efficiently and effectively as possible. Officers are also accountable for every round fired.

Wedge

Responders must always weigh the situation, location, resources available, and time allowed when picking the tactic to be used. In certain circumstances, it may be more practical for responders to use a large wedge formation. This formation is similar to the diamond formation used in hallways, but with more space between each responder. This technique can be used to cross large open areas quickly. Each responder will be responsible for a specific portion of the threat area as he or she moves. The spacing between responders is crucial to the element's survival, should they come under fire. The closer responders are to each other, the easier it is to attack several responders with one sight-picture and multiple trigger pulls. The farther apart responders are, the harder it is to attack more than one at a time. It is also important that the team move quickly to get out of the open danger area. A high speed of movement makes the team harder to engage accurately and also minimizes the time in which responders are exposed while crossing the danger area.

If a team is engaged by a suspect, the suspect should only be able to fire on one team member at a time. Other officers should have ample opportunity to see where the fire is coming from and respond accordingly because, with proper dispersion between responders, the suspect will only be able to get an accurate sight picture on one responder at a time. If everyone is grouped up, the suspect will be able to engage many first responders with a single sight picture.

Obviously, neither movement technique provides perfect protection for first responders. This is a reality of the response to an active shooter event. First responders may be shot. The goal is to make it as hard as possible for an attacker to engage the responders; the mission (stop the killing) must be completed.

Breaching into the Crisis Site

Breaching is quite possibly the most overlooked critical skill set a first responding officer can possess. Even after the events at Virginia Tech, where the shooter chained and locked the doors from the inside to slow down the inevitable response, breaching is still often overlooked or glossed over in training. Hundreds of thousands of dollars worth of training and equipment are rendered worthless if the responders cannot gain access to the attack site.

The breaching techniques in which most special operation units receive instruction are mechanical/manual, ballistic, high energy, and exothermic. For most first responding officers, the more exotic breaching methodologies (high energy and exothermic) are not an option. Very few, if any, patrol officers today can be found patrolling our neighborhoods and city streets with a Broco® torch or rolls of det-cord and blasting caps. This lack of highly specialized and expensive breaching systems is understandable when talking about first responding officer's capabilities.

However, there are few excuses for not carrying inexpensive and readily available mechanical/manual breaching tools. These mechanical/manual breaching tools in the hands of first responders, with minimal training, can defeat most locked or barricaded entry points into a building.

Ballistic breaching is another extremely effective method of breaching and requires little if any modification to existing shotguns in most law enforcement inventories. There are some inherent risks involved anytime a live firearm is discharged; however, when done correctly, ballistic breaching can be one of the most efficient breaching methods available to first responding officers. Ammunition selection and training from a credible training organization are all that is needed to prepare first responding officers to breach using this technique. Most reputable ballistic breaching courses being taught today range anywhere from 8 to 16 hours of instruction. Each of the breaching methods is discussed in more detail next.

Manual/Mechanical Breaching

Manual/mechanical breaching refers to methods where human-powered tools are used to force entry into a structure. Rams and Halligan bars are very effective for gaining access through doors or windows. These tools can be relatively expensive as well. Sledge hammers, FuBars, and pry bars are less expensive and can be almost as effective. Officers must be trained in the use of these tools if departments seek to maximize their breaching capabilities. Simply buying the tools will not automatically make someone a breacher.

First responders not only need to be capable of stopping threats with lethal force, but also need to be able to breach their way into a structure with these tools. Carrying these heavy tools can be difficult. Some thought and training regarding how these options will be carried and employed is essential. Slings can be attached to both the Halligan bar and the sledge hammer for ease of carry and to allow the officers to keep both hands on their weapons until the tools are needed. Most Halligan bars, in fact, have sling attachment points where a sling can be easily attached. A sledge hammer with a weight of 8–10 pounds can have the handle cut down to 18 inches and a sling attached for ease of carry.

Other tools like the Stanley® FatMax FuBar are excellent tools for emergency or first responder breaching. The 18-inch version will fit perfectly into a flashlight ring found on most officers' duty belts. These tools can be used both as a prying and striking tool and are easy to carry into a dynamic environment. The physical exertion of carrying this additional weight while tactically moving to and through a crisis site is something that should not be underestimated either. It is imperative that officers not only practice employing these tools, but also how they will carry these tools into and around the crisis sight (Picture 5.1).

Breaching tends to be associated with doors, but first responders should not limit themselves to doors alone. What if it is believed that an attacker has booby trapped the doors to a building or has set up an ambush point that covers the doors? In these cases, officers should consider making entry through windows or somewhere other than common entry/exit points of the building.

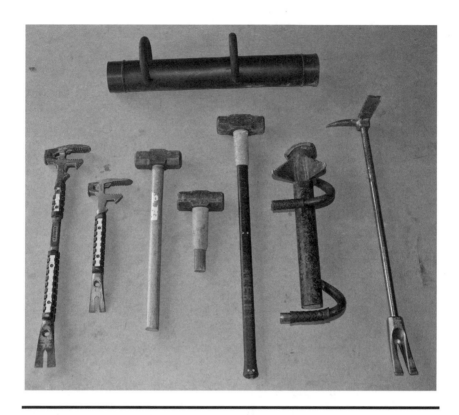

Picture 5.1 Manual breaching tools for first responders. (Top: Blackhawk's monoshock ram; left to right: Stanley® FuBar® forcible entry tool: 30 inches; FatMax® Xtreme™ FuBar™ utility bar: 18 inches; 8- to 10-pound sledge hammers, 24, 12, and 32 inches; BTI's Mity Mouse Ram; Paratech's Hooligan Tool, 36 inches)

It is much easier to gain entry undeterred or undetected if officers pick a window far away from common entrances than it is to work in or around the main entrances. The reason for this is twofold:

1. The offender has likely identified the most immediate or easily accessible entrances and created a plan to keep you out. It is relatively easy to control these main access points as there will be few of them. It is much more difficult to control all of the windows on a structure because

there will be many more of them. Consider the typical house. It will generally have only two doors, but there will be least a dozen windows.

2. The construction of doors and windows in the immediate area of a major access point into a building is usually very robust. Construction is stronger for a simple reason: security. These points are designed to keep people out. As you get farther away from that access point, the construction of the windows becomes less robust and is often ornamental. This makes these windows easier to defeat.

There are many ways to break windows. There are tools designed specifically for that task or improvised tools. There are tools that are expensive and those that are not. Essentially, responders need to use a tool that can effectively defeat the glass in question and provide stand-off distance from the impact area and the responder's hands. Much blood has been shed while simply breaking a window.

Windows can be broken and the shards of glass cleared out in anticipation of using them as breach points. Careful inspection prior to attacking the window may reveal a sliding window. In this case, it makes more sense and is faster simply to break the glass near the locking mechanism, unlock the window, and open it. This ensures that less pain is endured while crawling through.

In the extreme circumstances that surround active shooter events, first responders might also want to consider unconventional mechanical/manual tools or breach points. For example, the exterior walls on many structures may not be particularly strong and it may be faster to rip through the wall than breach a door. A vehicle can also be considered to be a ram that weighs several thousand pounds and will likely overcome an obstruction put in place by the attacker. Obviously, care must be taken not to harm the innocent and ensure that the entire structure does not collapse if this breaching option is utilized, but it may be a viable option in some circumstances.

When using a vehicle, consider using the trunk of the vehicle as the point of contact with the point of entry. This will minimize the damage to the engine compartment and will help to make sure that, once the breach has been conducted, the vehicle will be able to move out of the breach point. Airbags are also a consideration and responders should consult the vehicle manufacturer about the design of the airbag deployment. Some airbags will not deploy when the vehicle is struck from the rear.

Ballistic Breaching

Ballistic breaching can be achieved by using the standard buckshot issued to first responders who carry shotguns. Slugs are very effective as well when breaching, but can also potentially produce casualties on the other side due to the heavy slug still having a lot of energy after having gone through the retention system and the material the barricade is made out of. Slugs are actually too effective and can possibly cause more problems on the other side of the door than they fix. Buckshot will lose a great deal of its energy passing through a door or barricade and this serves to minimize the injury that could result should the rounds impact someone on the other side.

Specialized breaching rounds can also be purchased. These rounds are specifically designed to dump energy into the retention system and then turn into powder or dust. These rounds are usually made of compressed copper or zinc. They are specially designed to allow ballistic breaching to be used with the least amount of risk to lives on the other side of the breach point. These rounds are also very expensive because of their special nature and construction. Regardless of the specific round that a breacher will employ, training and practice are needed to make ballistic breaching as successful and safe as possible.

High-Energy Breaching

Most commonly known as "explosive" breaching, this method aims to use the smallest amount of explosive material necessary to breach into a crisis site. Knowledge of what these charges are made with, how they are constructed, and how they are applied to the access point is extremely important. This knowledge is important not just for responders who are using this method, but also for leadership so that they know what is being attempted and why.

When one says the word "explosive," it conjures up visions of mushroom clouds and smoldering debris fields where people and buildings once stood. The reality of this type of breaching is usually anticlimactic. An experienced explosive breacher can often successfully breach a door with a very small "explosion." Being familiar with what is involved in this process is key to knowing what it can achieve and, more importantly, what it will not do.

Due to the specialized nature of this type of breaching, it is unlikely that most first responders will have this capability. It is very likely that first responders can find themselves working around tactical unit personnel when these options are being utilized. Specialized units that do employ this method should make first responders aware of its capabilities and aware of what is involved with its application to minimize potential problems.

An explosive breaching alternative for first responders that is less complicated in regard to training, certifications, maintenance, etc. is the "wall banger." This piece of equipment takes the energy of a DefTec noise/flash diversionary device (NFDD) and channels it into the door that needs to be breached. It is very effective and requires less initial training and maintenance to sustain this program than a traditional high-energy breaching program.

A 1-day training on the proper use of NFDDs and then use of the wall banger system itself are sufficient to make first responders capable with the equipment. After the initial

Picture 5.2 Wall banger being deployed.

purchase of equipment and devices, minimal maintenance training will be required to ensure capability with the system. This system has proven that it can breach many obstacles standing in a responder's way up to and including class 3 metal doors that open outward. To be able to remove these barriers quickly and efficiently is vital in quickly stopping the killing of innocent people (Picture 5.2).

Exothermic Breaching

Exothermic breaching involves the use of heat to cut through doors or other barriers. A variety of tools are available to accomplish exothermic breaches, but most are some form of high-temperature cutting torch that can be used either to cut the locking mechanism or to burn through the door hinges. Becoming proficient in this type of breaching also requires training.

A Final Note on Breaching into a Crisis Site

Responders should keep in mind that it might be possible to stop the killing without breaching into the building. If information coming from inside the crisis site places the shooter in a room with exterior windows, officers might be able to stop the shooter faster by shooting the offender through an exterior window than by entering the structure. This can also be safer for the officers because they will not be forced to move through the door into the room that the subject is in. Stopping the shooter through a window obviously has its limitations and cannot be done on the higher floors of a structure, when there is a lack of credible information regarding the location of the shooter, or there is no/limited access to the room through a window; nonetheless, it is an option that first responders should consider before breaching into a building.

If responders choose to try to stop the suspect by shooting through a window, they should consider the effect of the glass on their rounds. It is difficult to predict what a bullet will or will not do after penetrating an intermediate barrier, such as glass, in the field. There are an enormous number of variables that must be considered. Issues range from glass composition to caliber of weapon; from angle of engagement to target distance from the barrier. Whole books have been written on this subject matter alone. It is recommended that officers experiment with firing through intermediate barriers using their duty weapons and ammunition in an attempt to get a baseline on their specific weapon and ammunition combination. Although not perfect, this should help officers understand the limitations they may face when firing through glass.

Chapter 6

Entry and Confronting the Threat

Introduction

The predators within our society who rationalize the murder of innocent people as a way to right some perceived injustice must be stopped. Unfortunately, all too often it is only after the slaughter has begun that the attacker's depraved intentions are fully realized. It is at this moment that the actions of first responders may be the only thing standing between the slaughter of the innocent and the monsters that perpetrate such acts. The more quickly first responders can get within range of the shooter, the more quickly the shooter can be removed from the equation.

The chapter begins where the last chapter left off. It is assumed that the first responders have arrived at the scene, moved up to the crisis sight, and breached their way into the building. We begin with the concepts and principles of team movement inside a structure.

Concepts and Principles of Team Movement inside a Structure

In Chapter 4, we discussed concept and principle-based training. In this chapter, we present the six concepts and principles of team movement that we teach in our classes. They are designed to be remembered and executed easily by the first responding officers. These concepts and principles are the following:

- Stay together as much as possible
- 540° Cover around the team
- Communication
- Cover the angles
- Threshold evaluation
- Speed of movement

Stay Together as Much as Possible

Most active shooters target locations with tens, hundreds, or even thousands of potential victims. Many of these potential victims will be trying to exit the attack location while the officers are trying to move into the site. Staying together will prevent the officers from potentially becoming separated and isolated if swarms of people are moving past.

By staying in close contact with other officers, it is easier to communicate with other members of the team. This is especially true when entering an environment where the ambient noise (such as alarms, screaming, gunfire, or explosions) could be a barrier to communication. The stress of responding may also cause *auditory exclusion* to occur, which may require that officers use nonverbal communication such as hand and arm signals or touch indexing to communicate. Communication is the key to efficiency of any team.

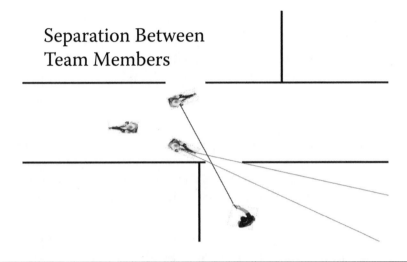

Figure 6.1   Improper separation between team members.

A team moving within a structure must constantly observe and cover angles that open and close. By staying close together, officers can cover angles that their teammates cannot cover but are exposed to. Figure 6.1 shows that when team members are improperly separated, the team may not be able to cover each other effectively. Figure 6.2 shows how the same threat is effectively covered when the team stays together.

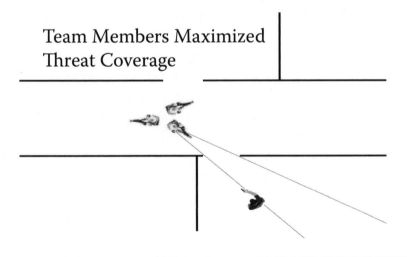

Figure 6.2   Team staying together.

A team that stays together can also maximize firepower on a threat quickly and efficiently. By staying together, team members will be less likely to fire over, around, or past each other to engage the threat, enabling officers to mass firepower safely on a threat in confined areas and at close quarters.

540° Cover around the Team

This concept recognizes the fact that most officers under stress will search for another human on a horizontal plane at eye level. In other words, when hunting humans, we search for them at eye level. This is not a problem as long as the gunman is standing. Many times, however, the person we are looking for attempts to gain a tactical advantage by taking up a position above or below eye level.

First responders should visually search from directly above their heads down to their feet and from side to side. First responders should train their eyes to focus into and at areas that can or could conceal a human, obstacle, or other dangers such as booby traps or explosives. Too often officers waste valuable time focused on areas where it is clear that none of these things exist or could be concealed.

Officers should focus on their primary area of responsibility, but should also overlap into their partner's area of responsibility. This will create a redundant system in the event something is missed or overlooked by one responder.

When actionable intelligence is causing the team to move directly to a known threat, 540° of cover around the team will allow it to bypass uncleared areas within a structure while maintaining a reasonable level of security. In a structure with numerous unknown persons, you will not be able to stop and investigate every person you come into contact with or every location that could possibly conceal a threat. This "dome of protection" around the team allows the team to move into the threat area to neutralize a known threat quickly while protecting the team from the unknown.

Communication

Communication is the most critical aspect of working as a team. There are very few problems in the world that cannot be solved by clear and concise communication; the remaining problems can be solved with the proper placement and application of high explosives.

Effective communication is the glue that holds the team together and ensures that, regardless of size, the team acts as one. Ineffective communication will turn a team into a group of individuals, often working in opposition to one another. The team will receive a great deal of information collectively, but this information must be communicated effectively so that decisions can be made. The ability to communicate can be improved with more training, situational awareness, familiarity with the priorities of work, and brevity codes used by officers who know that system of speaking.

It is important to think of effective communication as a communication *loop*. In order for communication to be effective, there must be a *sender* who gives information to the *receiver*. The loop closes when the receiver acknowledges the message and gives feedback to the sender. A sender who does not receive any feedback must immediately assume that the message was not received or understood. One should never assume that a message was received and understood if feedback is not received. Conversely, if you are in the position to receive a message from one of your teammates, it is imperative that you close the loop by giving him or her feedback. Sometimes feedback is nothing more than asking the sender to repeat or clarify a message. Many times, in training, officers take communication for granted and fail to train for communication problems. At other times, communication (or the failure to communicate) is overlooked as a possible reason for a team's effectiveness or ineffectiveness.

Types of Communication

Communication is typically broken down into two categories: verbal and nonverbal. Verbal communication is the spoken word. There are times during a tactical operation when verbal communication may not be the preferred method of communication, such as prior to making a room entry. In these instances, nonverbal communication such as hand and arm signals or touch indexing is appropriate.

Levels of Communication

Due to the complexity of the active shooter response, you must also communicate at different levels. The first level of communication is between members of the team. Team members should also communicate with witnesses or victims to gain valuable intelligence about the actor or actors. A third level of communication must take place between different teams of first responders working inside the crisis site. Linkup procedures must be worked out prior to friendly elements coming into contact with each other. The linkup will most likely start with verbal communication via radio; however, teams may conduct the actual linkup using nonverbal communication such as white light, hand and arm signals, or other signaling devices.

Barriers to Radio Communication

It is important to remember that an active shooter response is not normally a planned response. First responders will arrive on scene in a *first come, first respond* order. This may include first responders that do not work for the same agency or unit. The issue with radio interoperability was brought to the forefront during the terrorist attacks in New York on September 11, 2001. First responders could not communicate with each other. This problem still plagues the majority of first responders today. Buildings often become a barrier to radio communication. The thick concrete and steel walls of many structures can diminish the effectiveness of the best communication equipment.

In the chaos of responding to an active shooter scene, many officers will arrive without any radio communication. If practical, first responders without radios should partner with another first responder who has radio communication.

Cover the Angles

Teams of ten fail to effectively cover the angles during both training and operations. For example, officers on a team will watch one of their members go "hands on" alone with a suspect 10 feet in front of the team. The other members of the team will stay back and "cover" the hands-on officer, but the angles to which the handcuffing officer is now susceptible are not being covered adequately by the rest of the team. Also, the team will not be able to cover beyond the handcuffing officer without having to shoot uncomfortably close to or over the handcuffing officer. The only way to cover someone's rear end is to be on his or her rear end.

The urban battlefield is full of hard angles that officers must constantly identify and cover visually for as long as their team is exposed to the angles. When moving, either inside a building or on a city street, officers will constantly be exposed to an array of opening and closing angles along the route. As the team slows or stops, the angles of exposure remain open for longer periods of time. Responders must remain situationally aware of angles that pose a danger to the security of the team and ensure they are covered. Figure 6.3 shows angles of exposure to which a first responder is exposed on a common city block. The diagram only shows the exposures that exist at the corners of buildings. If exposures from windows, doorways, and rooftops were included, the numbers of angles of exposure would dramatically increase.

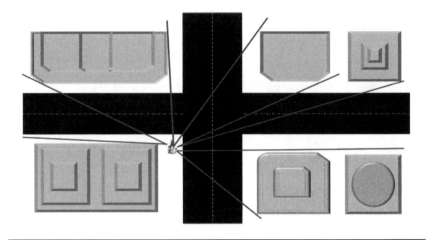

Figure 6.3 Angles of exposure.

In most settings, the first responders will not be capable of covering every angle of exposure at all times. First responders must learn to prioritize which angles should be covered more thoroughly than others. For example, when officers are moving down a hallway, they should prioritize angles by distance from the team. As a team passes an open door in a long hallway, they should cover the angles of exposure through the open door because of its proximity to the team. This will mean that, depending on the size of the team, officers may briefly have to drop observation of angles at a distance down the hallway in order to cover the angle that is closest to the team.

If the first responders become stationary, they should all assess their coverage areas to ensure coverage of angles of exposure. Depending on the floor plan, officers may have to reposition themselves slightly to cover the most immediate or dangerous angles of exposure to the entire team. This is especially true for the *rear guard*.

Threshold Evaluation

Also known as *slicing the pie,* threshold evaluation is a technique used to observe the majority of the room prior to entry. We recommend the *threshold evaluation* technique because most first responders do not have adequate training in dynamic entry techniques. Dynamic entry techniques are most commonly used by specialized, cohesive teams who train together regularly. Many first responding officers have limited or no training time together, making a well executed dynamic entry difficult if not impossible. The threshold evaluation technique also allows the team to gain vital information about the room, its layout, and its occupants in a more controlled manner than performing a dynamic entry.

It is not uncommon during active shooter events for individuals who are well trained and experienced in conducting dynamic entry operations to be on the scene of an active shooter with other responders who have limited or no exposure to or understanding of the basic concepts of an effective dynamic entry. Regardless of the finer points of dynamic entry, most operators who have been trained in and use dynamic entry operationally would agree that speed, surprise, and violence of action (or controlled aggression) are needed for a successful dynamic entry. In many active shooter situations, one or more of these principles is lost and this may cause a dynamic entry to end in catastrophe.

Once first responders identify a shooter in a room that they do not occupy, they have several options that they can explore. First, they can engage the shooter from outside the room through the threshold. This will normally also facilitate more than one first responder moving into a position to engage the shooter. If officers occupy the hallway moving toward a room of interest and can see the shooter who is murdering innocent people, what moves faster: bullets or responders? If officers can see up to 85% of a room through the threshold of a room, that means they should have a better than average chance of seeing and stopping the shooter without having to make entry and expose themselves to other possible threats inside the room. Picture 6.1 illustrates two officers performing a threshold evaluation and confronting a gunman.

Second, a single officer can enter just inside the threshold and stop to engage the shooter. This is often the most natural option for officers with limited training and experience in close quarters battle. Standing in the doorway happens frequently because officers are moving so fast that once they begin to enter a room and then identify the shooter, they stop to shoot. Although this may feel natural, it is *one of the most tactically unsound things an officer can do* in this situation. By stopping or pausing in the doorway, the officer makes himself or herself an easy target and makes it virtually impossible for his or her partners to assist because they are stuck outside the doorway with no way to safely engage past the initial officer.

Third, the first officer can trust that the other first responders are trained in dynamic entry techniques and enter the room, close distance, and engage the shooter inside the room. This is effective when, at a minimum, the first two officers know exactly what they are doing when they conduct the entry. Most ad hoc teams that form up and move to contact a shooter have limited to no training together and, therefore, this option may not be the best choice. When officers enter the room to confront the shooter, they put themselves into a new 540° problem and are also closer to the threat, making everyone's hit ratio go up, including the shooter's. Often, first responders will focus on the first threat they see and will not quickly, if at all, identify other threats inside the room. When multiple responders enter a room, oftentimes the less experienced trailing responders will get focused on what the first officer in the room is doing. The potential problem that this causes is illustrated in Picture 6.2.

Many officers agree that the first option, threshold evaluation, is probably the best option in most situations. The Advanced Law Enforcement Rapid Response Training

Picture 6.1 Using the threshold evaluation technique, officers are shown engaging the shooter from an area they control without exposing themselves to other possible threats inside.

Picture 6.2 Too often officers using a dynamic entry model without using threshold evaluation will focus on the first and most visible threat when entering the room, thus leaving them vulnerable to other threats.

(ALERRT) Center has reviewed tens of thousands of hours of officers during scenario-based training and found that even those officers who claim to be proficient in dynamic entry often fail to pick up a second threat inside a room. It is unfortunate, but many officers refuse to look at the problems with dynamic entry when used during an active shooter incident. Many say that, statistically, active shooters are typically single shooter events and, therefore, the dynamic entry will work. Although it is statistically true that most active shooter incidents involve a single shooter, officers should prepare for situations where two or more shooters are involved. We recommend following the "one plus one rule" that is taught in most law enforcement academies. Once you have found one bad guy, you should immediately start looking for the second. Domestic and foreign terrorist organizations train using paramilitary tactics where the minimum team used will be two; this is done for basic security needs. Training and tactics should always be evaluated against worst-case scenarios, not the most simple.

The threshold evaluation technique itself can be conducted more quickly when shots are being fired inside the room and, when done properly, can be effective in stopping a mass murderer. The technique narrows the officer's exposure to the room to approximately the same area as the visual field when under stress. The technique also aids in limiting "priority of fire" issues with one officer shooting past another to engage the shooter. Time spent in the hallway should be minimized, but the work that needs to be done while already in the hallway should be maximized. The team must be able to assess what they can from where they are prior to closing distance. At the same time, the team must be able to surgically engage a lethal threat while not hitting innocents.

The extra few seconds it takes to evaluate the room prior to entering can pay off immensely. Threshold evaluation is a simple way to maximize the limited time spent in the hallway just outside the room. While conducting the evaluation, officers should look for people and threat indicators while noting the layout of the room and potential threat areas that cannot be seen from the hallway. Officers must also be trained to look for potential hazards such as improvised explosive devices (IEDs). When officers use threshold evaluation, they are positioned to see possible explosive devices or triggering mechanisms before they make entry into the room. Due to the intelligence gained from using the threshold evaluation, they may elect not to enter and risk a possible detonation of the device. We cover IEDs in more detail later in this chapter.

Threshold evaluation is initially shown and practiced slowly. Again, this is done in order to learn how to do it correctly and is also done slowly in the context of a building search where little, if any, information is known. The pace is then picked up several notches once a driving force (e.g., gunfire) is introduced or when the skill level of officers increases to the point that the evaluation can be done effectively at a quicker pace.

Threshold evaluation is not a substitute for a room entry. Once a room has been scanned from the hallway and no threats have been detected or a shooter has been confronted and neutralized, a proper room entry must be executed in order to secure and clear the room. Room entries are discussed later in this chapter.

Speed of Movement

The energetic nature of the response to an active shooter can often overwhelm the senses of the first responder. It is imperative that the team responds quickly and efficiently to the sounds of gunfire. Moving "quickly" toward the sound of gunfire is not a natural act. In fact, for most people, to move quickly (or slowly for that matter) toward the sound of gunfire is counterintuitive; yet, with each shot heard, there is the possibility that someone has just been seriously injured or killed. Many officers, when told they must respond quickly, believe that they must sprint as fast as they can to the location where the shots are being fired. The murderer must be stopped, but officers cannot move so fast that they cannot process critical information and effectively understand the information that they are receiving in the context of the situation.

Officers should try not to move faster than they can shoot accurately and think. Most well trained officers will say that it is not the shooting accurately but rather the thinking that will determine the speed of movement. Shooting is a motor skill that, when properly trained into muscle memory, can be done very quickly and accurately. Thinking, or *situational awareness,* in a dynamic life or death situation can quickly overwhelm the best target shooter.

Mental preparation is just as important, if not more so, than any physical skill when responding to an active shooter. Just like any motor skill, first responders must train their minds to sift through and separate relevant from irrelevant information quickly. This can be done using mechanical methods in much the same way that we train the body to shoot by breaking down and understanding things like grip, stance, sight alignment, and sight picture. One method is mechanically to break down how we look at our environment in a high-stress situation.

The three most important things to look for in active shooter/close quarters battle situations are (1) people, (2) open angles of exposure, and (3) potential angles of exposure (i.e., closed doorways). When moving toward an objective, officers should be searching constantly for these three priorities. In most active shooter situations, there will be a large number of these priorities to assess. It is possible that there will be people everywhere, open and closed doorways, and 90° angles around walls and furniture, windows, vent openings, and open atriums. Officers must train to search mechanically through this array of possible threats and threat areas and sift out what is pertinent and what is not.

One example of this is how we look at people. We break down our *scanning sequence* of a person into a five-step mechanical process:

1. We look at the entire person. Is the person wearing a distinct uniform that marks him or her as another officer? Do you recognize this person as a noncombatant? Is the person postured and moving like another officer, a victim, or a shooter?
2. We look at the hands. Hands kill. Is the person that you have observed and identified as an unknown armed? If the person is armed, then officers must take whatever action is immediately necessary to make sure the person does not hurt innocent victims or officers. The officers' actions will be determined by the "totality of the circumstances" as the officer perceives them at that time.

3. If no visible weapon is in the hands, we scan the waist-band. An overwhelming majority of the world's population is right handed. Criminals and terrorists seldom, if ever, use holsters. Most weapons that are not visible will be tucked into the waistband between the navel and strong-side hip. This area should be scanned for any noticeable bulges. Since most criminals do not use holsters, they may also have a tendency to touch the area where the weapon is through their clothing to ensure that the weapon has not moved or slipped from its original position.

4. We examine the area surrounding unknown people. Officers under stress often experience visual narrowing or *tunnel vision*. When this happens, the officer will focus solely on the individual and can fail to see a weapon located in close proximity to the person. Officers must train to break the visual narrowing and scan the immediate area controlled by the person to make sure no weapon is immediately accessible.

5. We check the subject's demeanor if we are dealing with a small number of people. Officers should attempt to read the person's facial expression and body language to determine if the person is a potential threat. When having to measure the demeanor of a large group of people in a small confined area, it is best to start with general verbal commands with which everyone should be able to comply. Persons failing to comply with simple verbal commands should then be zeroed in on and their demeanor should be checked. Are they scared to death and frozen, or do they appear to be looking for the right moment to launch an attack on the team? The situation in general should be the final check. Is the person acting like a normal, rational person would be expected to act in a similar situation? If not, that person deserves extra attention.

At first glance, this scanning sequence may seem too slow. It is important for officers to remember that once you have made the decision and pulled the trigger, you cannot stop the projectile if the decision is wrong. Scanning the entire person and hands is by far the most critical and time sensitive part of the scanning sequence. The scanning sequence, done properly, will only take a fraction of a second and will help to make sure the decision made is the right one.

It is imperative that responders not only quickly recognize the threat but that they also act accordingly based upon the level of threat perceived. Quickly identifying and perceiving a threat and then failing to act can have devastating consequences. Waiting for a suspect to raise the gun in the officer's direction before using force is an unrealistic constraint that some in our society would have placed on first responders. Fortunately for first responders, the US Supreme Court recognizes the fact that "action is faster than reaction" and has not placed this fantasy world view on their actions.

There are inherent limitations on a person's ability to assess and respond to a perceived threat. An individual's reaction will always be slower than the action that prompted the response. World-class athletes have a typical reaction time of 0.25 to 0.50 seconds under optimal conditions. Research conducted with first responders shows that, under stress, reaction time can range anywhere from 0.50 seconds to over 4.0 seconds. A well trained adversary can fire up to 10 highly accurate rounds in less than 4 seconds—a lifetime in a gunfight.

On top of the physiological limitations, mental factors can affect reaction time. Uncertainty as to whether an action is legally within the first responder's right can slow reaction time. Hesitation is often caused by a lack of certainty. It is imperative that first responders become intimately familiar with state and federal laws, case law, and any policy, procedure, or rules of engagement (ROE) to which first responders are subject.

Following are some of the most pertinent cases in the United States affecting first responders and the use of deadly force:

- *Graham v. Connor* established the *objective reasonableness standard* for police use of force under the Fourth Amendment to the US Constitution.
- *Montoute v. Carr* affirmed the first responder's right to react to a threat before it manifests into an assault.
- *Plakas v. Drinski* ruled that the US Constitution does not require first responders to use all feasible (less lethal) alternatives to a situation where deadly force is justifiable.

Room Entry

Once responders have conducted a threshold evaluation of the room, under most circumstances, the room must now be entered and cleared. This is a coordinated action that requires commitment on the part of the responders. Transitions from the area that the officers currently occupy into unoccupied areas (such as moving from a hallway to a room) are particularly dangerous. These transitions are dangerous for two reasons. First, the officers will not be able to see the entire room until they enter. The officers therefore do not know if a suspect is in the room or where the suspect is located. Second, the suspect will know where the police officers must enter the room (i.e., the door). This allows the suspect to position himself or herself in a way that allows him or her to fire at the officers as they enter the room and before the officers know that the suspect is present.

While we pointed out many of the potential problems with dynamic entries when we discussed threshold evaluations, the entry into a room after a threshold evaluation has been conducted must be dynamic. That is, when the decision to enter is made, the entry must be executed quickly and aggressively. The points of domination discussed earlier are designated to put a maximum number of responders inside a room as quickly as possible. Responders should be positioned where multiple responders can safely and effectively engage a single threat without accidentally shooting a teammate in the process.

Once the threshold evaluation has been completed, the officer who conducts the evaluation should communicate, depending upon the layout of the room and the technique to be used, who should enter into the room first. This is done using simple hand and arm signals. Responders who use verbal communication to develop this plan are violating the element of "surprise" and should be prepared for a failed entry if a suspect is inside. Once the order of entry has been communicated and agreed upon, the number two officer will wait for the number one officer to begin moving toward and through the threshold. The second officer must begin to move almost simultaneously with the first officer; this ensures that a minimum of two officers are quickly moving into the room and to their points of domination. If more than two officers are moving into the room, the additional officers will move into the room behind the first two officers and take up their points of domination. The first two officers inside the room are the most critical and this must be a coordinated effort.

For years now, there has been this great debate over exactly how the entry should be conducted. This is often referred to as the "known versus unknown" debate. This debate is centered around the idea that most rooms in American architecture are "L" shaped (i.e., the doorway is offset to the left or right of center). When encountering these rooms, three of the four corners, or over 80% of the room, can usually be seen from outside the threshold of the doorway. This leaves only one corner (referred to as the blind corner) where a person could be positioned with an unobstructed view of officers entering the room.

The advantages/disadvantages of the known and unknown entry techniques have been the subject of intense debate. The most common arguments will be summarized here.

In the "unknown technique" the first officer to enter into the room moves directly to the corner that cannot be seen or cleared from outside the room. This is represented by line 1 in Figure 6.4. The second officer into the room moves along

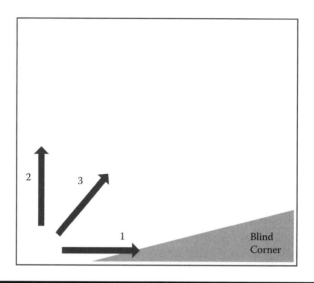

Figure 6.4 The great debate.

line 2. Supporters of the unknown technique argue that this gives the first officer into the room the best shooting accuracy because the officer is moving directly toward the threat and the threat is becoming a larger target as the officer advances. The belief is that accuracy is more important than other issues because the officer can best protect himself or herself by shooting and disabling a hostile suspect as quickly as possible.

The "known technique" subscribes to the idea that the first officer through the door should move in the direction of the corner that is visually cleared from and directly in front of the threshold. This is represented by line 2 in Figure 6.4. The second officer to enter the room moves along line 1. Supporters of the known technique argue that the unknown technique has several disadvantages. The first is that because the suspect is waiting in the room, he or she will be able to fire before the entering officer because the officer has to enter, scan for threats, assess the threat, decide to shoot or not, and then shoot, while the suspect simply sees a police officer come through the door and shoots. Reaction time research supports this contention (Blair et al. 2011).

The supporters of the known technique argue that this means the first officer must assume that he or she will not fire first and instead should be concerned with making the shots of the suspect less accurate. The lateral movement, relative to the suspect in the corner, is assumed to reduce the accuracy of the suspect's shots. Relatedly, supporters of the known technique argue that the shot accuracy advantage created when the officer moves directly toward the suspect in the unknown entry also applies to the suspect. That is, the suspect gets more accurate as the first officer in the unknown entry advances along line 1 in the diagram. The first officer in the unknown entry is believed to be more likely to be hit and be hit more often than the first officer in the known entry.

Second, critics of the unknown technique argue that, because the second officer to enter the room must move behind the first officer (through the suspect's field of fire), the second officer might be hit by shots intended for the first officer. That is, misses on the first officer (or bullets that overpenetrate and pass through the first officer) could become hits on the second officer.

Third, critics of the unknown technique argue that because the second officer must move behind and far enough past the first officer to fire safely, the second officer will be slower to fire at the suspect. This is important because the second officer must disable the suspect in the event that the first officer is disabled upon entry.

The primary critique of the known entry is that this entry reduces the accuracy of the first officer to enter the room. The argument is that while the lateral movement of the officer reduces the suspect's accuracy, it also reduces the officer's accuracy. This has led some critics of the known technique to refer to the technique as the "rabbit" because the purpose of the first officer is to draw the fire of a hostile suspect while the second officer disables the suspect.

To further complicate the issue, Paul Howe, a tactical training provider and former Special Forces operator has introduced a new technique. We refer to this technique as the *hybrid* because it blends elements of the other techniques. In this technique, the first officer moves along line 3 in Figure 6.4. The second moves along line 1.

Supporters of the hybrid technique argue that it possesses the strengths of both the unknown and known techniques. The slightly lateral movement of the first officer is believed to reduce suspect accuracy while not reducing officer accuracy. The entry of the second officer along line 1 is believed to be faster than the entry of the second officer along line 2 in the unknown entry and also not to expose the second officer to fire aimed at the first officer.

Data from our research suggests that the lateral movement in both the known and hybrid entries reduces the accuracy of suspects. The accuracy of police officers was not affected by the type of entry. However, the speed with which the first officer to enter the room fired was slower in the known entry than in the other two.

Regardless of the technique responders choose to use when making room entries, one thing is for certain. A successful room entry's foundation is based around a minimum of two committed individuals working in concert to enter the room as close to simultaneously as possible. In our experience, first responders fail to execute effective room entries successfully for a number of reasons:

1. *Fear or lack of commitment:* First responders must be totally committed to entering into the room. Room entries are one of the most dangerous situations facing first responders. They must be committed to moving into the room and occupying their *points of domination.* Fear is a natural response; first responders must control it and not allow it to control them. They must turn fear into controlled aggression and take the room like they are stealing it…because that is what they may have to do! This fear is related to a lack of proper mind-set and confidence in capability.

2. *Failure to dominate the room as a team:* A successful room entry will require two or more first responders entering as close to simultaneously as possible. The decision as to which responder enters first is not relevant if the second responder does not immediately move into his or her point of domination in the room.

3. *Failure to communicate:* Communication is the key to any successful tactical operation. A first responder who is going to launch himself into an uncleared room should make every attempt to ensure that at least one other responder is clear on his intent and the entry is a coordinated event. This can become a huge safety issue, especially when it comes to ad hoc teams.

4. *Failure to clear respective areas of responsibility:* It is human nature to look at things we perceive as threatening. In dynamic room entry, first responders must fight this natural tendency to look into an area covered by someone else prior to clearing their primary area of responsibility for any immediate threats. It must also be stated that responders must not continue to stare at an area that has been visually cleared. This slows down the process of scanning the room.

5. *Overpenetration into the room:* Overpenetration into a room can be just as dangerous as a lack of commitment to enter and clear the room. First responders who overpenetrate a room full of unknown persons can easily find themselves in a cross fire situation if a threat manifests itself. Too often, first responders train in sterile environments with threats that have already manifested prior to the team's entry into the room. Overpenetration will shrink responders' "fields of fire" inside the room and potentially position them in lethal cross fire situations.

6. *Moving too fast:* Aggression and violence of action are required elements of a successful room entry, especially when someone intends to challenge your actions. However, you must use controlled aggression

administered professionally and reasonably. Too often responders move too fast to *see* what they are looking at. It sounds counterintuitive, but slowing down a little speeds up the process of correctly "seeing" what is happening instead of just moving around a lot and "seeing" very little.

7. *Failure to recognize a threat:* Threat recognition prior to feeling hot lead and copper burning through your flesh at over 1000 fps is something all first responders should strive to achieve. Room entries are as much a visual exercise as they are a physical skill. Use the scanning sequence and *see* what you are looking at. Do not waste time looking into places where you know a threat is not or cannot be.

8. *Post-threat tunnel vision:* Neutralize the threat and then scan. Make sure there are no other threats present and make sure your partners are still standing, or in the room with you, before you scan back to the threat. Most importantly, make sure you neutralize the threat before starting your scanning sequence.

9. *Arrogance:* Room entry is a perishable skill. Just because a first responder attended a dynamic entry course 5 years ago does not make him or her an expert. Seek out reputable training, train on your own, or, better yet, with other first responders with whom you are likely to be working. Use visualization every time you walk into a room. Visualize points of domination and secondary threat areas. Program your "hard drive" every chance you get. Seek out new ideas and methodologies. A wise man once said, "We can stand around all day and pat each other on the ass, telling ourselves what a fantastic job we have done, when no one challenges us in the poor tactics we use."

10. *Lack of a combat mind-set:* First responders must develop and maintain a combat mind-set to be effective in the art of room entry. In room entry, your mind-set should be, "I hope the suspects are in here." With this mind-set, you

will never be surprised when you find the threat. You will be mentally ready and act accordingly. However, if your mind-set is, "I hope the suspects are not in here" and you enter and find them standing there, your first response will most likely be to freeze physically while your mind formulates a response. This could be your last action ever.

Keys to Effective Room Entry

■ **Speed.** Entry must be done quickly. Moving slowly will allow the opposition to see what is about to happen and create a response for it. Many times responders go faster than they can process information and stimulus. They never see the threat before the threat starts to engage the officers. Responders should slow down when learning a new skill or having to multitask on the move. The more training that is conducted, the better that responders will get at reading situations, anticipating circumstances, and responding correctly.

■ **Violence of action.** "Making believers of nonbelievers"—this is not an out-of-control rage, but "controlled aggression." People can look at and listen to the responder and know that he or she means business. If someone is moving and interacting with everyone in the environment as if he or she were scared to death of everything, not only will that not inspire confidence in the ability to save others, but it may also push those who are contemplating violence against you to act. Looking and sounding in control and confident can send a message to the fence-sitters that they should not try anything stupid.

■ **Surprise.** "Not knowing what was going to happen next"—this important factor seems to be the one that is most overlooked. Oftentimes, first responders will push a mission quickly and aggressively without really knowing or evaluating whether or not the element of surprise still exists. Unfortunately, we have seen, many times over recent years, what happens when very capable and qualified teams of officers have been met with a hastily planned ambush because the element of surprise was not present. No matter how fast or aggressive you are, if surprise is lost, you are merely quickly and aggressively moving into someone else's ambush.

The Room Entry Process

The traditional room entry process is to gain a flash site picture, clear the immediate threat area, clear corners, conduct primary scan, and conduct secondary scan.

- **Flash site picture.** To gain a *flash site picture* of the room means to take a snapshot of the room as one comes up to and into the doorway. This is done to look for any obvious threats (people with guns) that may be in clear view—looking for people or where people could be.
- **Clear the immediate threat area.** The officers must clear away anyone around the entrance that would prohibit the responders from entering. This means anyone standing too close for comfort to the door that responders are entering needs to be moved (if unarmed) or engaged with lethal force (if armed). This allows for the entire team to push into the room and take control.
- **Clear the corners.** Different schools of thought exist on this process. Some methods teach physically moving to the corner and standing in it to verify that it is clear. Other methods teach that if you can see the corner is clear from where you are, you can continue moving to your point of domination in the room and also begin your primary scan.
- **Move to a point of domination.** Officers must move to points in the room where they have made space for

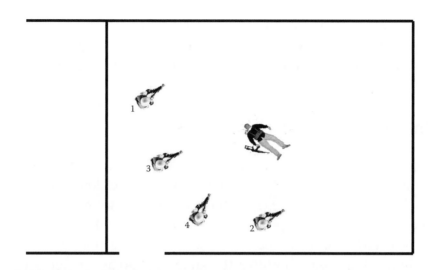

Figure 6.5   Points of domination. Illustration of officers at their points of domination inside the room. Notice the overlapping fields of fire that maximize the ability of the team to mass fire on a threat while minimizing the potential for blue-on-blue engagements.

follow-on responders to enter the room, can provide lethal coverage of the room in conjunction with others, and are not in a position where they may be hit by friendly fire if gunfire does erupt. All threats or potential threats should be in front of the team, making a 180° battlefield. This is illustrated in Figure 6.5.

■ **Conduct a primary scan.** The purpose of this scan is to ensure no immediate threats are present. Each officer should look from where he or she is standing all the way across the room until he or she can see another responder on the other side of the room. The primary concern of this scan is people. If a person is found, he or she must be scanned to ensure this person is not armed.

■ **Conduct a secondary scan of the room.** This is done to recheck areas that were not obvious concerns in the initial seconds of coming into the room, but could contain a threat. If any people were encountered in the room and were not considered an "immediate threat," the secondary scan is a time when verbal commands can be given to them to assess their compliance and give them direction.

Improvised Explosive Devices

The threat of explosive devices being used in conjunction with an active shooter attack is nothing new. In the Columbine High School assault, the perpetrators' plan was to initiate the assault with an improvised explosive device (IED) in the cafeteria during a lunch period. The investigation of the Columbine assault found that the attackers had assembled 99 IEDs including everything from small hand-delivered devices to vehicle-borne devices.

The terrorists who conducted the Beslan, Russia, and Mumbai, India, assaults also used explosive devices. First responders must prepare for this level of threat in their planning and training cycles. Standard *bomb threat* training will do little against an armed and murderous group determined to murder as many innocent citizens as possible.

In training first responders, we have found that IED scenarios are the most difficult for our participants. Knowing when to hold, go, or pull back in these scenarios is challenging.

Effects of an Explosion on the Human Body

The effects of an explosive device can vary depending on the type and size of the device. Nonetheless, explosions will affect first responders both physiologically and psychologically. When devices are used in an enclosed area such as a building or a vehicle, the *shock wave* is usually the most deadly part of the explosion. The shock wave travels in much the same way as does electricity or water; it will take the path of least resistance. Linear danger areas, such as hallways, should be evacuated as soon as practical prior to detonation of a device. The shock wave of a large explosion can disrupt and even destroy vital internal organs. Injuries from an explosive device will often include hemorrhaging from the nose, the ears, and even the eyes.

Refuge from an Explosive Device (Distance, Angles, and Air Gaps)

First responders must remember that if they can see the device, the device can hurt them. It may not always be practical for first responders to turn tail and run just because they located a device. Responders may have to continue pressing the fight if innocent persons are being murdered. In a hallway, take refuge by using *angles,* breaking 90° away from the device and entering a room prior to detonation if possible. If you locate an IED inside a room, move any victims from the area quickly and create an *air gap* (void space or buffer zone) between any hostage holding area or casualty collection point and the room housing the device. Prior to forcing victims to move, ask them if there is any reason they cannot move such as booby traps or devices attached to their bodies.

If a victim states that he or she has been booby-trapped or has had a device placed on him or her, attempt to keep the victim calm by explaining that specialists are on the way to help as other victims and responders evacuate the immediate area. If it is not practical to evacuate the building, take up a barricaded position using angles and air gaps.

While there is much discussion in police training and administrative circles about how to deal with homicide bombers, first responders should immediately deanimate a bomber on an active shooter scene. Never touch people suspected of having an explosive device; treat them like an explosive device themselves, because they are. Administer surgical headshots to the nasal cavity, ear canal, or brain stem. Handcuff them with lead and copper; do not touch.

Three Rules for Dealing with Explosives

Rule 1: Never touch the device. First responders who encounter an explosive device should never touch it. Also, take great care when touching anything that could possibly house an explosive device if reports indicate that actors possess or have used explosives during the assault.

Rule 2: Create distance, angles, and air gaps between you and the device. First responders who identify an explosive device should immediately seek refuge using distance, angles, and air gaps. If innocent people are being murdered, first responders may have to move past a device in order to close distance and neutralize the shooter. If first responders identify the device as using a burning fuse that has been lit, seek distance, angles, and air gaps until the device detonates. Remember: "If you can see the device, it can hurt you."

Rule 3: Communicate to teammates and incident command. Communication is key to survival in all aspects of responding to an active shooter. It is especially critical when dealing with explosive devices. If it becomes necessary to move past a device, communicate the presence and location of the device to teammates. The rear guard, upon notification, should immediately turn around and locate the device.

Common Types of Detonators Used with IEDs

Burning fuse. The simplest form of fuse is the burning fuse, believed to date back to tenth century China. The fuse consists of a burning core coated with wax or lacquer for durability and water resistance. The core of the fuse can be burning up to 6 inches beyond where you see the coating burning.

Booby trap. Explosive booby traps are designed to kill or incapacitate personnel. They are normally placed to avoid detection and are usually activated when an unsuspecting person disturbs an apparently harmless object or hits a tripwire. Booby traps can be placed to deny responders access into certain areas of a building and are normally found at choke points such as stairways, hallway intersections, and entry points.

Radio frequency/command detonated. Radio frequency (RF) detonated devices (also known as command detonated devices) are the least common types of devices currently found by law enforcement in the United States. Most explosive ordnance disposal (EOD) personnel have never encountered an RF detonated device outside a training scenario. It is important to be aware of these devices and their characteristics. Many terrorist bombings in the Middle East use a command detonation. These devices can be detonated by a signal from a mobile phone, pager, or any number of electronic devices that transmit a radio frequency or electronic pulse. This type of device is relatively easy to assemble and the components are easy to acquire.

Hand-Delivered Devices Used against the Team

Most hand-delivered (thrown) devices are small and designed to maim or kill persons. Most are composed of a low-yield explosive that will generate a pressure wave of less than 50,000 psi—more than enough to cause damage, although much less than a high-yield explosive's potential pressure wave of 4,000,000 psi. The shock wave consists of highly compressed air that travels outward from the source at supersonic velocities. When the shock wave encounters a surface that is in line of sight of the explosion, the surface reflects the wave, resulting in a tremendous amplification of pressure.

As seen in the Beslan, Russia, incident, terrorists used fragmentation devices against the Spetsnaz responders who assaulted the building in an attempt to rescue the hostages. Some devices were set up as booby traps and others were hand delivered. Rescuers found themselves in a delicate balancing act of push, hold, back up, and charge through as these devices were being deployed. The rescuers knew that simply yelling, "Bomb!" and pulling out was not an option. Explosions or not, the victims inside that school needed to be rescued and that meant the fight pressed on.

It is important that first responders develop tactics to counterassault a suspect who is using explosive devices. The following tactics are presented as a last resort, to save innocent persons and neutralize the suspect. Team members must be able to communicate details rapidly about the device and the action that should be taken by members of the responding team.

Bomb Cover and Bomb Go

We teach two techniques to address hand-delivered devices: Take cover or continue to close distance with the perpetrators and engage them. The momentum (or perceived momentum) propelling the hand-delivered device toward the team will determine which tactic the team should use.

Bomb Cover

Responders should call, "Bomb cover!" if it appears that the device being thrown at the team will stop at least 15 feet or more from the team's current location. When this command is given, team members should immediately seek cover wherever they can find it.

If team members attempt to find cover by exiting the hallway and making entry into a room, it is important to clear the room. It is natural for first responders to want to look at what they perceive as a threat to their safety. First respond-ers in training are often observed staring at the device now present in the hallway as they begin the process of leaving the hallway. In doing this, they pay no attention to the room they are entering as they seek cover from the device in the hallway. First responders must train to transition immediately from the threat of the device to making a proper room entry, and be prepared to address any threats while conducting the room entry.

Due to the dynamics of an explosive device being thrown at the team, each responder must be prepared to enter and clear a room by herself or himself. The responder's focus must quickly shift from the device to the room. Once inside, the responder should move to position himself or herself with his or her back against a wall and scan the room for any immedi-ate threats. This will decrease the threat angles, making the room more manageable for a single person to clear.

The responder should clear the room quickly and then get down as low as possible behind something that will stop shrapnel or secondary projectiles. If possible, the responder should not lie down, because it is difficult to fight from this position if fighting is necessary. The first responder should seek to reduce potential damage from overpressurization by rotating his or her weapon-side ear down onto the shoul-der, placing the weak or offside hand over the other ear, and opening his or her mouth.

After the device detonates, the first responder should move immediately to evaluate the threshold to the location that the responder just left. The responder should attempt to take a position inside the threshold to engage the suspect throw-ing the device. This can be accomplished in a number of ways. Remember that all threat areas must be covered; get as many weapons covering the threat areas as possible. If all first responders on the contact team have sought cover on the same side of the hallway, it is important to send two first responders (minimum) to clear a room on the other side as soon as practical. This will help provide effective cross cover down the hallway in the direction from which the IED came. Communicate to secondary responders so that they may attempt to neutralize the bomber from outside a window or other area. **Once an explosive device has been used against the team, members of the team should limit their movement away from covered positions.**

Bomb Go

First responders should call, "Bomb go!" if the energy propelling the device toward the team will carry the device to within 15 feet of the team, into the team, or through the team. When the "bomb go" command is given, responders should move quickly past the device and into a position to engage the suspect throwing the device.

This may require members of the team to enter a room with the bomber in order to neutralize the threat immediately. Great debate has taken place over neutralizing a bomber. Explosive devices do not discriminate regarding who they maim or kill. A person controlling an explosive must be neutralized before any body movement can occur. This can only be done in a timely manner by administering headshots to the suspect. Once neutralized, treat the bomber like an explosive device. **Do not touch.** Evacuate unknowns from the area, create distance (angles and air gaps), and communicate.

Reference

Blair, J., Pollock, J., Montague, D., Nichols, T., Curnett, J., Burns, D. 2011. Reasonableness and reaction time. *Police Quarterly*, 14, 323–343.

Chapter 7

Postengagement Priorities of Work

Introduction

Most first responders are *type A* personalities. They are mission driven, competitive, aggressive, and impatient. Many would say this is exactly what is needed for an effective response to an active shooter event; however, first responders must also temper their aggressive and impatient characteristics.

Many times in training, first responders will move to and neutralize the shooter, and then immediately move to find another unprovoked gun battle elsewhere in the structure. A type of *video game effect* takes over and responders begin to neglect necessary and vital training issues; their response seemingly becomes, "Okay, we have neutralized this shooter; level 1 is over, so let's move to level 2."

Not only is this unrealistic, it is also potentially dangerous for all involved. First responders must have a system to handle the issues created by the attack after they neutralize the immediate threats. After neutralizing a shooter, first responders must then neutralize the flow of adrenalin that is rushing through their bodies and begin to take actions that will help prepare them to act if another attacker is present or stop the dying of those who have been injured. Sometimes it will be best for the first responders to stay where they are and render medical aid before moving to another location. Other times, the circumstances may demand that the first responders leave injured people in order to deal with another threat. First responders must train in situational awareness and priority of work until they become second nature.

First responder training for rapid response to an active shooter scenario not only must include the initial response to isolate, distract, and neutralize the shooter, but also must train the first responder for the aftermath of the incident, so that the responder is properly prepared to stop the dying. This training should stress three priorities of work once the killing has been stopped: security, immediate action plan, and medical (SIM).

Security

Whether it is the ability to secure a specific location, an entire area, or just to keep security in one's immediate area, security is the first priority. Nothing else can be accomplished if the area is not secure. Maintaining the security of the team is the primary focus of the concepts and principles taught by Advanced Law Enforcement Rapid Response Training (ALERRT).

Once the shooter is dealt with, first responders must prepare themselves to take immediate control of the situation. The scene can range from chaotic to eerily silent. The responders to the Virginia Tech massacre reported that when they entered the rooms on the second floor, they initially thought that everyone inside was dead. The students, both wounded and not, lay so still and lifeless on the floors of the classrooms that it appeared there were no survivors. Only after the victims were sure that the threat was over would they move or communicate. First responders to other active shooter scenes have reported that the victims nearly overwhelmed them as they responded.

Regardless of the scene, first responders must immediately gain control over everyone in the room. Responders should not get in the habit of assuming who is good and who is bad. They should treat everyone as unknown until they have been thoroughly searched or vetted through a reliable source. Tell unknown persons in the room to do something once; if they do not comply, make them comply. Four or five first responders in a room with 15, 20, 30, or more unknowns can be easily overwhelmed if they do not exert positive control quickly and effectively. Pay attention to the behaviors and demeanors of the unknown people in the room. If someone stands out, give him or her extra attention until you have the situation sorted out.

There are two factors that weigh heavily in determining what can be accomplished and when it can be accomplished: time and resources. How much time the situation allows a team to work a problem is not known. How many resources are available to a team will depend on a few key factors. The first is what the first responders brought with them, and the second is what follow-on responders bring to the scene.

First responders should attempt to handcuff or otherwise secure any known shooters as quickly as possible without giving up security. Before attempting to secure the shooter, the team should move unknowns to positions of disadvantage using verbal commands. This will provide the team with more security while dealing with the downed shooter(s).

This also brings up the issue of who should be handcuffed. Some argue that everyone should be cuffed. This position is often not realistic in an active shooter event. If a team has four officers, each of whom carries two sets of handcuffs, what are they going to do once all eight pairs of cuffs have been used, and they have not even made it out of the first room yet? This issue can be addressed in two ways. First, the officers can bring more cuffs. Bringing more cuffs, preferably plastic flex-ties, which can be applied to "unknowns" encountered during a response, is a way to add more resources to the response. Iron cuffs on confirmed suspects and plastic ties on "unknowns" can also delineate between the two for sorting later on. Time also plays a factor. How much time will it take to handcuff/flex tie everyone inside a large structure with 1,000–2,000 people in it? The other solution to the handcuffing question is that only confirmed suspects get handcuffed and everyone else who is listening to directions will be handled using other methods. These methods are discussed next. This is obviously not an ideal solution, but the circumstances present at most active shooter events rarely allow for perfect solutions to be implemented.

One effective way for dealing with a room that contains both a downed shooter and unknown people is as follows. First responders should move unknown persons against a wall (called the *dirty wall*) inside the room and place them in a position of disadvantage (on their knees with their faces against the wall and hands on the backs of their heads) until the team can restrain the known shooters. This process also accomplishes another objective called *geographic triage.* First responders should quickly assess the casualties who failed to move against the wall and decide if any immediate life-saving intervention is needed once the suspects are restrained. Next, a quick assessment of whether the room is secure or not must be made. Completely processing a room takes a substantial amount of time and can result in victims bleeding to death from wounds that are treatable. During the "security" phase, first responders should not get caught up in having to do everything perfectly. One team member can hold cover on the unknown people in the room while another applies immediate life-saving medical adjuncts to a person who is within seconds or minutes of dying, for example. If it is believed that any other security issues are present, then those issues must be dealt with before beginning medical treatment. More on this will be covered under the "Medical" section.

If no other exigent circumstances (such as sounds of gun-fire or people in need of immediate medical aid) are known, first responders can begin *cleaning* the unknown persons inside the room. That is, the first responders can search the unknowns to ensure that they do not pose a threat to the victims or first responders. One method first responders can use to expedite this cleaning process is for the first respond-ers to clean two of the unknowns and then enlist these "clean" people to assist by identifying others that are not threats. First responders should clean anyone who they believe is suspicious.

With the unknowns moved against the "dirty wall" and placed in a position of disadvantage, the first responders in the center of the room should act as *cover* while the first responders on the perimeter of the room act as *contact* or *hands on*. The person who goes hands on should holster her or his weapon when cuffing or searching suspects to avoid potential negligent discharges. If there are four first responders in a room, with one covering hallway security, the responder in the center can cover while the responders on the outside move to contact. If there are only three first responders in the room, then the first responder in the center can act as the cover and the outside two first responders can operate as contact as hallway security is dropped. "Closing down" the room in this fashion allows for maximum security and open fields of fire in the event that someone becomes hostile. The hands-on first responder should immediately put his or her weapon back into a ready position after securing or searching the hostile or unknown.

Immediate Action Plan

After the team neutralizes all known threats inside the room and gains positive control over the room's occupants, they should formulate an immediate action plan as quickly as pos-sible. This actually may occur before the handcuffing process takes place. Responders might not have the amount of time it takes to process a room full of people adequately during a rapidly evolving multiple-attacker threat situation. If life is threatened elsewhere, the team should have a well thought out and communicated plan to ensure an efficient response to the new threat.

The responder who assesses the room and determines that he or she should turn and provide cover on the hallway through the doorway should also communicate the team's status (location, injured, killed in action, etc.) via radio to the command post or other responders. This will start the process of situational awareness, which will aid in the immediate action planning process.

After completing the status update, someone on the team needs to decide upon a course of action in the event more gunfire erupts and the team needs to move to another location to defend innocent lives. It will usually come from the responder holding hallway security or whoever is on the radio. Knowledge of what is happening outside the team's immediate area affects the plan, so it is logical that the one with that knowledge should develop the plan. The immediate action plan should be simple, easy to understand, and based on a when/then model such as, "When *<this event>* happens, then *<team member name>* will stay here and *<team member name>* will move to the threat." This should be the first phase of the immediate action plan and responders should develop it as soon as is practical.

The immediate action plan helps to minimize confusion among teammates if the situation dictates that the team must suspend postengagement operations in one room and move to another location to stop the murdering of innocent persons. The K.I.S.S. principle (keep it simple, stupid) applies here. There is no need to develop a five-paragraph operations order to give each first responder a general task assignment. A simple statement like, "When shots are fired, you stay; we will go" is best. It is imperative that all responders involved in the plan give feedback indicating that they heard and understood the plan.

An immediate action plan should take into account the *totality of the circumstances* as they are perceived at the time. For example, if there are known to be five other contact teams moving inside the crisis site, first responders may not want to leave the location they are working. They may elect to set up a blocking position in a hallway and allow another team to move to the second crisis point.

It may not always be possible to leave a responder at the current scene while others leave to confront a new threat. With smaller teams, all responders might have to leave a scene in order to effectively stop the killing somewhere else. First responders should consider several factors and be prepared to justify why they took the actions that they did. In many states, the law requires first responders to safeguard offenders once they are in custody. If first responders secure a shooter and then leave to respond to another shooter, and the victims turn on the restrained shooter and beat him to death, first responders need to articulate why they were unable to safeguard the shooter they had taken into custody.

First responders should also consider the team's capability before moving to a second crisis point. If members of the team were wounded during the entry into the room containing the shooter, the team may not be able to move to deal with a new threat. Once the immediate action plan is established, it is time to initiate the medical portion of the SIM model.

Medical

First responders' number one goal when responding to an active shooter scene is to stop the shooter or shooters from murdering unsuspecting victims as quickly as possible. In most circumstances, the actor or actors will have injured and/or killed numerous persons before the initial first responders arrive on scene.

Most civilian emergency medical service (EMS) personnel are not trained to work in high-risk, life-threatening environments where an active threat exists. Under most circumstances, EMS will stage several blocks away from the incident and not enter the scene until it is declared secure. In a large structure or during events where a number of conflicting descriptions of the shooter are given out, the process of searching the crisis site to ensure that it is secure can take hours. Life-threatening injuries require immediate medical intervention in order to increase the chance of survival. Every second delayed may reduce the likelihood of a favorable outcome. Therefore, first responders must be trained in basic combat medicine, so that once they have stopped the killing, they can administer basic life-saving techniques to *stop the dying* and stabilize victims long enough to get them to higher levels of medical care (Picture 7.1).

First responders should address medical issues as soon as they establish security and formulate the immediate action plan. First responders should attempt to communicate with follow-on responders and guide them into the team's immediate area of control. It is important to remember that, depending on the overall situation, a follow-on team may not be available for an extended amount of time.

First responders should carry a minimum of three wound kits each. Wound kits consist of simple life-saving items designed to control bleeding and treat gunshot wounds. If wound kits are not available, first responders should use field expedient items to treat the wounded.

First responders in most circumstances will still have to provide security. It is difficult to provide first aid and security at the same time. First responders may consider enlisting the help of uninjured victims to administer first aid. This will allow the first responders to stay focused on security while also providing treatment to the injured. Allowing

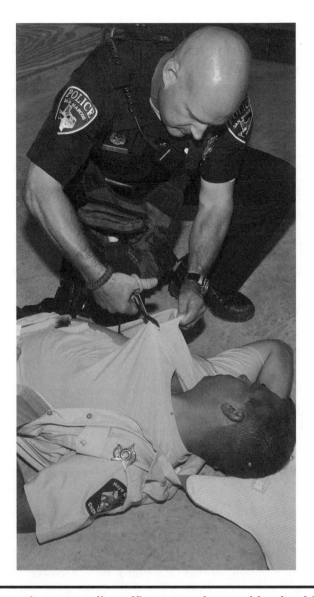

Picture 7.1   First responding officers must be capable of stabilizing critical patients prior to EMS arrival on the scene.

victims to assist rather than sit helplessly and watch events unfold can also aid in their psychological recovery. Victims that are dead should be covered or removed from the immediate area if practical. It is also important to remember that the scene is a crime scene and should be preserved as much as possible. The best set of medical guidelines for first responders to follow in active shooter situations was developed by the Committee on Tactical Emergency Casualty Care (CoTECC) and comes from lessons learned on the battlefields of Iraq and Afghanistan. We discuss these lessons and guidelines next.

Tactical Emergency Casualty Care

War and conflict drive advances in trauma care. Historically, the gap in knowledge transfer from the battlefield to the civilian medical setting is significant, up to 10 years by some accounts. However, extensive and aggressive medical data collection coupled with advanced technology on the battlefields of Iraq and Afghanistan, has allowed for more rapid integration of lessons learned. While we have seen the integration of these important lessons to some extent in civilian trauma centers, only small advances, mostly in an ad hoc fashion, have been appearing in the prehospital setting.

Tactical emergency medical support (TEMS) has a long and storied history in the United States. During the last decade, enormous progress has been made in developing professional and operational standards within the field. However, to date, there still exists no set standard of care within the TEMS specialty. Additionally, current civilian first responder practices and principles do not adequately address the need for *point-of-wounding* care in emergency response. Rather, civilian standards continue to emphasize scene safety and casualty evacuation while ignoring care rendered.

These same gaps existed in military operations prior to the mid-1990s. In response to operations in Somalia, medical providers within various military Special Operations Forces (SOF) examined the causes of combat-related deaths as well as the manner in which medical care was being delivered in the field. The conclusion was that the broad application of civilian trauma principles in combat often negatively affected mission success and appropriate casualty care. This deficiency led to the creation of the doctrine of Tactical Combat Casualty Care (TCCC) within the Special Operations community.

Over the past decade of war, TCCC has expanded from SOF into the conventional military and is now considered the standard of care for prehospital trauma care on the battlefield. The Committee for Tactical Combat Casualty Care (CoTCCC) and TCCC have been credited with reducing the case fatality rate (CFR) in current combat operations from approximately 14% in Vietnam to 9.2%–9.6% during Operation Iraqi Freedom and Operation Enduring Freedom.

The proven success of TCCC has led the civilian medical community, both tactical and conventional, to examine closely the tenants of the TCCC doctrine and integrate portions of the doctrine into civilian trauma care. However, the lack of a coordinating body has resulted in a fragmented and inefficient transition. There exist some fundamental differences between military and civilian high-threat care in terms of the population of patients, available resources, liability, and common language. The successful translation and application of TCCC principles in the civilian setting require a close examination of these distinctions. The CoTECC was convened to address the unique operational gaps specific to medical care and rescue initiated at the point of wounding. The Tactical Emergency Casualty Care (TECC) Guidelines are a set of best-practice recommendations for casualty management during high-threat civilian tactical and rescue operations. The TECC guidelines are based upon the principles of TCCC, but account for differences in the civilian environment, resource allocation, patient population, and scope of practice. TECC has three goals:

Prevent further casualties. The threat should be dealt with before running to the aid of injured persons. More often than not, the rescuer becomes a victim if the shooter has not been isolated, distracted, and/or neutralized before the responder renders aid.

Treat the casualties. Once the known threat has been neutralized, isolated, or distracted, immediate life-saving intervention should be a priority. First responders are also expected to remove themselves from the threat area (often referred to as the "X") and treat themselves if they are capable.

Complete the mission. The greater good of accomplishing the mission, especially in a mass casualty incident, is more important than any one individual. In an active shooter event, this means that the killing must be stopped. A successful Beslan or Mumbai style terrorist attack will mean an increase in attacks across the country. American first responders must demonstrate to the terrorists that what they perceive as a *soft* target really is not.

The CoTECC defined the phases of care following the model of the TCCC with language added to clarify the phases for high-threat, civilian tactical emergency medical response. These phases are discussed next.

Care under Fire/Direct Threat Care

Direct threat care is treatment rendered at the scene of the injury while both the caregiver and the casualty are under hostile fire. Available medical equipment is limited to that carried by each responder and the medic.

The best medicine during care under fire/direct threat care (CUF/DTC) is to stop the attacker from causing more casualties. This means that the injured party/team should actively engage the suspect. If this action kills the suspect, thereby rendering him or her incapable of inflicting any more casualties, medical treatment can be administered in a much more controlled manner. If this does nothing more than distract the suspect and prevent him or her from engaging first responders with well aimed fire, this too is achieving the goal of stopping the shooter from causing more casualties.

The "point of wounding" or the exact location of the responder when hit is referred to as the "X." The suspect has proven that he or she can hit responders in this area and the first responder should immediately move off the X. This may require responders to return fire as they move. Responders should seek positions of cover or, at minimum, concealment from the shooter. If the injured cannot move themselves from the X due to the extent of the wounds inflicted, responders should use coordinated directed fire at the suspect before a rescue is attempted. Any rescue attempted prior to isolating, distracting, or neutralizing the shooter will more than likely end in failure with more responders wounded and in need of rescue.

The primary goal of CUF/DTC during an active shooter response remains the same: STOP THE KILLING. As long as the gunman remains at large, responders' number one goal is neutralization. As a first responder, there are times when actionable intelligence about the exact location of the shooter does not exist. Security must remain high but certain medical adjuncts can be utilized in an attempt to stop the dying of victims. The only authorized medical adjunct used during CUF/DTC is the tourniquet, which is used to stop excessive hemorrhaging from an extremity. The only other medical treatment that should be done during this phase is placing the wounded, especially the unconscious, into the "recovery position" (Picture 7.2).

During the past 10 years of military conflict, the US military has validated the use of tourniquets as a primary hemorrhage control method, and proper tourniquet application is credited with saving countless lives. Unfortunately, the opposite is true

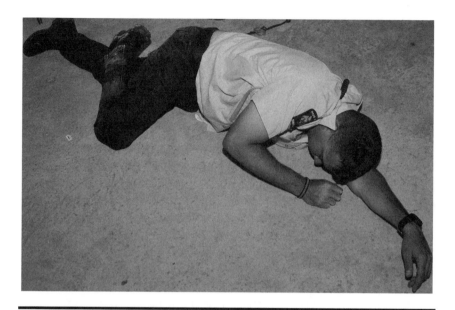

Picture 7.2 Simple procedures like placing victims into "recovery position" can assist victims medically and help follow-on responders recognize victims who have been assessed.

as well. The reluctance to use tourniquets on major extremity hemorrhages in civilian medicine has resulted in deaths that were later deemed preventable. There is currently a push by first responders across disciplines to train all first responders in the proper use of tourniquets. More and more first responders can be seen carrying tourniquets while on duty. The tourniquet is a simple medical adjunct that dramatically increases the ability of first responders to "stop the dying."

Tactical Field Care/Indirect Threat Care

Indirect threat care is rendered once the casualty is no longer under direct hostile fire, but there are still potential threats in the area. Security must be maintained, but because the team is not under direct fire, additional medical interventions are appropriate in this situation. In addition to the tourniquet and recovery position, the additional medical interventions provided at this phase include applying occlusive dressings to wounds in the chest cavity area and bandaging injuries in other areas. Medical equipment is still limited to that carried into the crisis site by first responders and improvised from within the environment.

It is important for first responders to know and understand basic bandaging skills in addition to tourniquet application. In the event the victim cannot be quickly extracted, all preferred care options will fall back on the first responder to perform. Wound packing has been a topic of much debate and, under normal circumstances, should be left to medical professionals. However, when medical professionals are in short supply and the situation is anything but normal, a first responder with quality training and a simple understanding of how to pack a wound properly can save lives. It is important to remember that the lives being saved using the skills may also be the lives of other first responders.

A seriously injured victim can easily require more than one first responder for treatment. In addition to the process of locating and assessing the wound(s), the need to access the proper equipment and prepare it to be applied is important and may require an extra hand. Some of these treatments may require first responders to help control the victim during treatment. Packing a wound on a victim that is conscious and feeling pain can be a difficult process. It can easily take three people to work on one seriously injured victim. Time and resources will often dictate just what can and cannot be accomplished given the circumstances.

It is also important to remember that the time from when known threats have been neutralized until evacuation may range from a few minutes to many hours depending on the situation. In a mass casualty situation, such as was seen in Mumbai, India, in 2008, the sheer number of casualties can quickly overwhelm most emergency medical systems. Evacuation from the crisis site and the provision of higher levels of medical care may be considerably delayed. Properly applied care at the crisis site can dramatically increase the survival odds of the wounded.

Tac-Evac/Evacuation Care

Evacuation care is rendered just prior to and during the evacuation of casualties to higher levels of care. Additional personnel (such as tactical medics, paramedics, and EMTs) often become available during this phase of care. The additional personnel will usually bring additional medical equipment.

To improve evacuation care, the wounded should be consolidated in a casualty collection point (CCP) when it is practical to do so. The CCP should be a room capable of housing all the victims with injuries requiring medical treatment. This may be a series of rooms next to each other if the number of casualties far exceeds the space available in the room. Establishing this point has three primary advantages:

1. Because the wounded are consolidated in one location, security is easier to establish and maintain.
2. Better triage decisions can be made. Triage involves grouping victims by the severity of their wounds (and thus how immediate their medical needs are). If the person in charge of triage can see all of the victims, he or she can make comparative judgments about the need for care. A variety of triage systems are in use in different jurisdictions. At ALERRT we use a simple two category system. Victims are classified as IMMEDIATE or DELAYED. Victims with life-threatening injuries are classified as immediate and everyone else is delayed. If one room is used, the casualties are separated into immediate and delayed groups. This can be done by writing "IMMEDIATE" on one wall of a room and "DELAYED" on an opposing wall. As casualties are brought into the CCP, the person in charge of the room will inquire as to the category of the patient and then direct the patient

to be placed in the appropriate area. This will aid the medical personnel in their assessment of the most critical patients and assure they receive attention first. If multiple rooms are used for this purpose, mark one of the rooms as "IMMEDIATE" and the other "DELAYED" and have the patients placed into the rooms in accordance with their category. It is also important to remember that casualties inside the CCP, both IMMEDIATE and DELAYED, should be constantly reassessed until evacuated to a higher level of medical care.

The medical system can be easily overwhelmed and first responders should do their part to limit the amount of chaos heading into the system. The walking wounded will normally self-evacuate to medical aid and will more than likely be the first ones to arrive at the hospital. Most of these victims do not have life-threatening injuries. There are a finite number of ambulances in any jurisdiction; therefore, it is important that the most critical are evacuated first. If first responders do a poor job of triage and just start shuffling anyone with an injury into the first available ambulance, the most critical will be the last to go and be much more likely to die.

Responders must understand that, to the victim who has just sustained a non-life-threatening gunshot wound, his or her injury is the most important injury in the world and requires immediate treatment. This is often not the case. It is the victim that cannot talk or move due to penetrating trauma to the torso that most often needs immediate care.

Responders also must not add to the chaos by using their patrol cars to transport victims with non-life-threatening wounds. This not only fills the hospital with less critical patients, but also takes away from the security elements on the scene. If responders do not work in a coordinated effort with Fire and EMS providers, the most critical will be the last transported and will be delivered to a hospital in chaos.

3. Treatment is improved. Using a CCP and having all the victims in close proximity to each other will aid tactical medics and other medically trained professionals who enter the crisis site by allowing them to treat and continually assess their patients without having to expose themselves to possible threats inside the structure. One paramedic or tactical medic can triage, treat, and continue assessment of a large number of patients if the patients are in one location. This will be much more difficult if victims are scattered throughout the crisis site.

The CCP can also be used as a consolidation point for all medical equipment either carried into the scene by responders or scavenged from the environment. If each responder carried the equivalent of one "ALERRT Victim and Responder Kit" (Picture 7.3) on their person when entering the crisis site, there would be enough medical equipment initially to treat and stabilize a large number of victims. If responders do not train and establish a protocol to consolidate medical equipment, most of it will remain with responders as they conduct security missions and the critical medical equipment will not be used.

Picture 7.3   AVAR kit contents.

CCP Location

The placement of the CCP will be determined by the circumstances of the situation. As mentioned previously, time and resources will be important. The first factor in selecting a CCP location is whether or not the officers present can secure the location. If they cannot, the location is not suitable for a CCP. Additionally, limitations in manpower may create a situation where the officers cannot move victims from their location to the CCP while maintaining adequate security at the CCP and along the transportation route. This means that the first responding officers, in many circumstances, will create an initial CCP in the room where they engaged or found the shooter and will only be able to provide care to the victims in that room. As more responders arrive, it will often be possible to consolidate more victims in the CCP or to move the CCP to a better location. Where possible, the CCP should be established as close to the evacuation point as possible. Anytime that a victim is moved, first responders should reassess the casualty's wounds. Tourniquets and bandages should be rechecked to ensure that they are still properly positioned.

It is important to remember that the purpose of the CCP is to provide immediate life-saving care to victims and to triage the wounded so that medical resources can be applied effectively. The CCP is only temporary, and the focus should be on getting victims who need higher levels of care to that level of care as quickly as possible. We have sometimes observed, during training, that officers become so focused on providing a textbook CCP that they spend a large amount of time moving victims from one CCP to another within the attack site—when manpower at the time was enough to stabilize the wounded and provide adequate security to move the victims from the attack site directly to the CCP that was established by EMS outside the immediate threat area.

A Note on Blast Injuries

With the possible use of IEDs or other explosive systems, treatment of blast injuries can add complexity to an already difficult scene. In addition to the obvious trauma that can be expected, many people can suffer major internal damage if close enough to a device when it detonates. The signs of these injuries can be very difficult to detect. A person may look perfectly fine one moment, but then lose consciousness the next. First responders need to know that people close to a blast or detonation who show no visible signs of injury should be considered as potentially injured.

Linkup Procedures

It is generally during the "stop the dying" phase of active shooter response that the attack site will be flooded with first responders. It is important to recognize the danger that this poses to both the first responders already in the attack site and the secondary responders entering to help. The potential for friendly fire "blue on blue" incidents is high.

Teams of first responders must establish positive communication before coming together. As described earlier, a responder inside who is able to communicate over the radio the location and situation of the team will aid in this process. Linkup can begin over the radio by gaining situational awareness.

Secondary responders should not enter into the area controlled by the initial contact team until communication with the contact team is established. Linkup protocol must be established and understood before the secondary responders enter.

Contact team members should attempt to *mark* their exact location inside the crisis site. They can accomplish this using terrain designation such as, "We are inside the third room on the right once you enter the doorway, room 212." Another method is for the contact team to use a device to mark the team's location. This might be the use of a chem-light or small battery-operated strobe light. If none of these devices are available, first responders can use field expedient items to mark their location, such as chairs stacked on top of each other outside the doorway or trashcans in the center of the hallway.

Contact team members should not be in the hallway when the secondary responder team is given permission to enter. This is done to prevent the creation of a cross fire situation if a threat comes out of a room between members of the secondary responder team and contact team (see Figure 7.1).

If for some reason this does occur, it is important to remember that the *moving* team has priority of fire. This is almost always the secondary responder team. Members of the contact team should evacuate the hallway or make themselves small to avoid being hit by friendly fire.

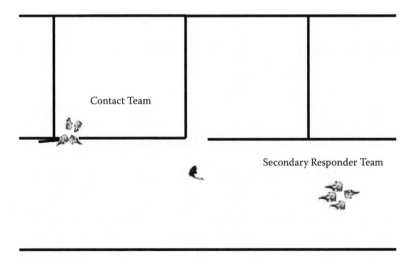

Figure 7.1 The moving team has priority of fire; watch for cross fire situations during linkup.

Priorities for Incident Commanders during the "Stop the Dying" Phase of Response

In all likelihood, incident command will not be established until the shooter has been neutralized and the focus has shifted to stopping the dying. During the initial part of the stop the dying response, the situation will be extremely chaotic. Existing intelligence is likely to be weak, and incoming reports will often contain contradictory information. The number of shooters will be unclear. First responders will be swarming to the site and asking for direction. Incident commanders must not allow the uncertainty and chaos to paralyze them. Mistakes will be made. When they are, they should be corrected as quickly as possible and the response should continue.

Often, everything will seem like a priority, and since no two situations are ever exactly the same, it is difficult to lay out clear guidelines that are easy to follow and apply to every specific situation a leader may face. The following is a list of priorities that apply to most active shooter scenes. It is designed to be used as a general guide:

- Provide security and quick reaction force.
- Clear evacuation route for victims.
- Establish a casualty collection point.

Provide Security and Quick Reaction Force

Security is always the top issue and should never be forgotten or abandoned for some other perceived priority. As a leader, you should always be thinking about security. Security covers an array of different topics. The security of officers and innocent victims should be the top priority when at an active shooter scene—especially a scene that has not been secured and may conceal other threats.

Individual officers will develop their own set of priorities and, if allowed, will act on them. Some will be in perfect alignment with what should be done and others will be outside the responder's current capabilities and/or resources. There is a phenomenon often seen in training where officers, as soon as the known suspect is confronted and neutralized, immediately want to move to the next room and clear it of any possible threats. They will step over dying role players in the hallway to get into that next room and clear it. Although the next room does eventually need to be cleared, without the actionable intelligence driving officers to clear the room immediately, there are other priorities that should be considered before the next room is cleared. It is the role of the leader to step in with a set of priorities that fit the mission. Stop the killing and then stop the dying.

Officers often explain their actions as wanting to clear the other rooms because of security concerns. "There may be another shooter in the other room, and I don't want them to sneak up on me and attack when we are most vulnerable." This line of thinking is not totally out of line, and for this reason we should always consider our security as a first priority. But what happens when we leave the immediate area where we have confronted and neutralized one shooter, and multiple victims lay dead and dying on the ground? What happens when we find nothing in the next room? Do we continue to search for this possible second shooter until the entire building is cleared? If so, what happens to those innocent victims who were shot by the suspect and required life-saving intervention? Do our actions help us to meet our goal of stopping the dying?

When a team focuses on establishing security, they will be prepared for any unknown threat that may attempt to sneak up and ambush them. A team that establishes an immediate action plan will be prepared to move out of the area they currently occupy immediately, if need be, and address any new threat once that threat is actually known to exist. Meanwhile, follow-on officers will be responding to the scene and the team can continue with security measures and treat any victims that need immediate life-saving intervention, thus meeting both goals of stopping the killing and stopping the dying.

The incident commander should establish a quick reaction force that can immediately enter the crisis site and deal with any new threats that arise. This team should consist of four or five members. The incident commander should position this team in a location that will allow for both quick access to the crisis site and clear communication between the commander and the team.

Clear Evacuation Route for Victims

Once enough officers have entered the scene to provide security and a quick reaction force, the next priority should be to clear a route for evacuating both injured and uninjured victims from the building. An exit point must be identified, and then a route (or routes) from the location (or locations) of the victims must be cleared and secured. The exit point should be chosen based upon the location of the victims and to facilitate the ability of ambulances to get in and out of the attack site. In general, the shorter the route is, the better, unless the shorter route creates security concerns. Multiple exit points may have to be established, but this can present problems. If two evacuation points are established, it is more difficult to triage victims effectively and more officers are required to clear the routes and provide security.

Once the exit point is chosen, officers must search all of the rooms along the exit route to ensure that no additional threats exist. After the route is cleared, officers must continue to provide security along the route. Blocking positions should be established at locations where the exit route is connected to other areas of the building (such as hallways and exits).

Establish a Casualty Collection Point

Establishing a CCP was discussed in detail in the medical section of this chapter. The incident commander must know where the officers have set up their initial CCP(s) and use this intelligence to decide whether the existing situation is acceptable or whether a different CCP should be established. Commanders should always keep in mind that the purpose of the CCP is to triage victims and get those who need higher levels of medical treatment to that treatment as quickly as possible.

Chapter 8

Civilian Response to Active Shooter Events

Introduction

The rest of this book has focused on describing active shooter events (ASEs) and suggesting how the police can best respond to these events. In this section, we turn to some suggestions about how civilians can best respond to these attacks. We begin by discussing the role of civilians during ASEs. Next, we discuss the basics of how people react in life-threatening, disaster situations. After that, we discuss the specifics of how to identify and respond to an ASE, and, finally, we present a very simple policy example to help those who are attempting to draft their own policies.

The Role of Civilians during Active Shooter Events

While our analysis of active shooter events clearly shows that the police play an important role in limiting the casualties that occur during an active shooter event, the actions of the police are only part of the picture. Recall that, on average, it took police an average of 3 minutes to arrive on scene and an additional several minutes to locate and stop the shooter. This means that for at least the first several minutes of an attack, the potential victims are essentially on their own.

We view the number of casualties (defined as people shot or killed) during an attack as being a function of two things: (1) the amount of time that the shooter has to perform the attack, and (2) the rate at which the offender can find suitable targets to shoot. More formally, the equation is something like this:

Casualties = f(rate of suitable target location*response time)

The time that the offender has to commit the offense is primarily how long is takes the police to stop the shooter. The rate at which the offender can find targets is primarily the result of two things. The first involves the design and usage of the attack location (how many people are there, how densely they are concentrated, and how quickly the offender can gain access to the subareas of the attack location). The second is the behavior of the potential victims at the target location.

This section focuses on the behavior of potential victims. The data on ASEs in Chapter 3 showed that about half of all attacks end before the police arrive. The data show that many times the attack stopped because the potential victims took action to stop the shooter directly or made it difficult for the shooter to find targets. Our belief is that the actions of civilians can dramatically affect the number of casualties that occur during an attack. Civilians who are well prepared to respond to an attack can save not only their own lives, but also the lives of others. We turn now to discussing the basics of how people respond during life-threatening disasters.

Disaster Response

In her excellent book on disaster survival, Amanda Ripley (2008) identifies the common response patterns of people in disaster situations. She argues that three phases of response are commonly seen. These are denial, deliberation, and the decisive moment. Each of these stages is discussed next.

Denial

Contrary to the common perception of people panicking and stampeding during a disaster, Ripley (2008) found that it was more common for people to deny that the disaster was happening. The investigation completed by the National Institute of Standards and Technology (NIST) (2005) into the collapse of the World Trade Center towers on September 11, 2001, found that, on average, people on the lower floors of World Trade Center 1 waited 3 minutes to start evacuating and those closer to the impact floors waited an average of 5 minutes before they started evacuating. The occupants often indicated that they spent this time speaking to others about what was happening and gathering belongings. Clearly, this delay could have led to many more deaths had the fires caused by the impact been more severe or spread more quickly.

When the people did start evacuating, they did not panic and stampede (NIST 2005; Ripley 2008). They moved purposefully to the fire exits and left in an orderly fashion. This is despite the fact that they had heard an enormous explosion that shook the building and the presence of smoke and fire on many of the floors.

Ripley (2008) argues that this denial is rooted in the normalcy bias. That is, our brains tend to interpret information as if it is part of our everyday experience. Because of this, people tend to underestimate both the likelihood of a disaster and the possible effects of the disaster. It takes time for the brain to process the novel information and recognize that the disaster is a threatening situation.

It is also possible that this response is rooted in the phenomenon of social proof. Cialdini (2008) identifies social proof as the tendency to look to other people for cues about how to behave in novel or ambiguous situations. In a disaster, this means that people would look to each other for information about how to act. If most people are calm, the group will tend to remain calm. If others are panicking, that panic will tend to spread. This has important implications for the information presented later in this chapter. A single prepared individual can help set the tone for the group and save their lives. Whatever the cause of the denial phase, once the denial is overcome and the person realizes that the situation is threatening, the deliberation phase begins.

Deliberation

At this point people in a disaster have to decide what to do. If the person does not have a preexisting plan, this creates a serious problem because the effects of life-threatening stress on bodily systems severely limit the ability to perceive information and make plans. Next, we provide a brief overview of the effects of life-threatening stress on a person's ability to think and respond

What Happens under Stress

Psychologists generally view the brain as having two different modes of thinking or systems (Kahneman 2011). These are typically called system 1 and system 2. System 1 responds unconsciously, automatically, and effortlessly with little sense of control. System 2 is responsible for conscious activities like controlling attention or developing complex plans. System 1 also corresponds to older, more primitive brain structures (think reptile brain or emotional brain), whereas system 2 corresponds to more modern brain structures (think human brain or rational brain). All animals have a system 1. Humans have the most developed system 2 of any animal. System 1 is much faster than system 2.

System 1 constantly monitors incoming sensory information to determine what information should be passed on to system 2 (Kahneman 2011). Because we are concerned about dangerous situations in this section, we will focus on potential threats and unusual information (unusual means unknown and unknown is inherently threatening to system 1). Because system 1 plays a significant role in the survival of all animals, it tends to be biased toward false positives. System 1 would rather treat something as a threat and be wrong than to ignore it and be wrong (LeDoux 1996). If it is not a threat and you react, the cost is generally small (such as flinching and being a little embarrassed). If it is a threat and you did not react, the cost could be your life. If a potential threat is detected by system 1, this information is sent directly to your amygdala, which manages your fear responses. Your amygdala will begin immediately and automatically to respond to the potential threat. This occurs before you are even consciously aware of the threat.

At the same time that system 1 has detected a potential threat and sent information directly to the amygdala, system 1 will also send the information to system 2 for further assessment, and this assessment is then sent on to the amygdala (LeDoux 1996). When the information reaches system 2, you become aware of the threat, can assess it, and decide what further action is needed (if any).

If someone jumps out from behind some bushes and screams at you, your system 1 will probably classify this as a potential threat. This information will be sent directly to your amygdala, and your amygdala will immediately begin to respond. You might flinch, for example. The information will also be sent to your system 2 for processing. If system 2 decides that it was just your friend playing a joke on you, it will send a stand-down message to your amygdala, and your body will begin to return to its normal state. If system 2 decides that the potential threat is someone who is actually attacking you, system 2 will not call off the system 1 response; rather, it will let system 1 continue to ramp up your body's threat response. System 2 will also begin to consider the available courses of action (the most easily available of which will be the automatic ones suggested by system 1) so that you can decide what to do.

The threat response system controlled by our amygdala can be seen as a series of alarms that progressively marshal more and more of the body's resources as they are set off (LeDoux 1996). The fastest of these are the least discriminating and easiest to trigger. A loud noise, for example, may activate our startle reflex (which might cause us to flinch). If the loud noise was not a threat, this reflex action is wasted, but in cases where the noise is a threat, the startle reflex starts the process of getting us ready to act. As the series of alarms are activated, more and more of our body's resources are focused on the threat. Heart rate, breathing, and blood flow to the large muscles all increase to prepare us to act physically. The machinery of the brain increasingly focuses on the threat. The immune system also ramps up in preparation for injury. These physiological changes allow us to use our body's machinery to its fullest extent during times of crisis to respond physically to a threat. The changes make us faster, stronger, and more focused (Grossman 2008).

This process is largely under the control of system 1. The further down the stress response trail one moves, the more impaired system 2 becomes because system 1 activities are taking up more and more of the body's resources. As stress mounts, the ability to think decreases. Given enough stress, everyone loses the ability to think rationally (Grossman 2008). Research suggests that, under stress, people default to actions that are preprogrammed into system 1 (Staal 2004), even if these actions are not optimal. For many people, these actions are limited to fighting, fleeing, or freezing.

The ramping up of your survival machinery also produces a variety of side effects. Officers involved in shootings or other violent encounters have frequently reported the following side effects (Artwohl and Christianson 1997; Klinger 2009; Pinizzotto, Davis, and Miller 2006).

- Tunnel vision: your field of focus may narrow to only the most immediate threat and you may not see peripheral details.
- Audio exclusion: you may stop hearing what is happening.
- Time dilation: things may seem to move in slow motion.
- Out-of-body experiences: you may feel as if you are outside your body watching the event happen.
- Reduced motor skills: you may experience reduced efficiency of your fine motor skills.
- Loss of bladder and bowel control: you stop monitoring the state of your bladder and bowels, and if there is urine or excrement, it comes out.

These are all side effects of your stress response system preparing your body to deal with a threat. These system 1 responses to threats developed during a time when the most likely threat was going to come from a source that needed to be dealt with physically and immediately—a tiger jumping out of the bushes in front of an early human, for example. The human needs either to fight it or to flee. The threat environment faced by people today is often much more complicated. For example, you might need to find an alternative exit or perform fine motor activities like dialing 911 for help. The following sections discuss techniques to keep system 2 functioning longer and how to prepare to act when system 2 is compromised.

Keep System 2 Functioning Longer

- **Use willpower.** Willpower can be simply described as using system 2 to override system 1. In the case of a disaster, system 1 is setting off a variety of panic alarms. By exerting willpower, a person is trying to get system 2 actively to override these alarms. This can be done, but it takes conscious effort. Willpower is also a limited resource. Willpower can prevent or delay some stress responses, but it will eventually fail.

- **Breathe.** Combat breathing consists of breathing through the nose for three counts, holding the breath for two counts, breathing out for three counts, and then pausing for two counts before beginning the next breath. The use of this technique has been shown to lower people's heart rates dramatically for a short period of time and can help to circumvent some of the system 1 alarms (Grossman 2008).

- **Take care of yourself.** Research has shown that people who are more fit are also generally more able to cope with stress (Staal 2004). Part of this gain may be due to a fit person's regulatory system being better able to deal with the physiological swings caused by stress, and part of it may be due to willpower. Most people do not like to get up in the morning and go work out. The act of exercising requires a use of willpower. Forcing yourself to go work out on a regular basis may create increased willpower reserves. Improved diet and sleep habits can also reduce your base stress level and improve your ability to function in critical situations. Think of it this way. If your operational ability is impaired when you reach a 10 on the stress scale, and you walk around in daily life at a 7, it does not take very much before your ability to function is reduced. If, however, you reduce your base stress level to a 2, you can handle a lot more before stress begins to reduce effectiveness.

■ ***Habituate to likely stressful events.*** Being exposed to situations that are similar to real-life events makes them less stressful when actually encountered (Grossman 2008; Saunders et al. 1996; Staal 2004). This exposure helps prevent some of the brain's alarm systems from firing, and this can dramatically reduce overall stress reaction. The more realistic the training is, the better the habituation effects on stress response become. Training should simulate, to the maximum extent possible, the situations that are likely to be encountered. This will help keep system 2 functioning when critical events are encountered in real life.

■ ***Act.*** Freezing often leads to feelings of helplessness. When people feel helpless, their stress levels increase and this further impairs functioning. Taking action, any action, can help give some sense of control and help reduce stress response. Acting also gives the brain something to do other than focusing on the alarm signals that are being set off.

What to Do When System 2 Is Compromised

No matter how much willpower you have, how good your physical conditioning is, or how much you have habituated to particular stressful situations, you will run into situations where system 1 overwhelms system 2, at least for short periods of time. You need to prepare for this. Next are a few tips to help function in these situations.

■ ***Shift the emotion.*** When system 2 has overwhelmed system 1, it is easier to overcome one system 1 function with another than it is to restore system 2 functioning. When experiencing feelings of panic and fear, it is easier to shift the fear response to anger than it is to restore control. Do not get scared. Get mad at the offender!

■ ***Prepare critical skills to work when system 2 is not functioning.*** One of the great things about system 2 is that it can create new programs for system 1. System 2 is actively engaged when a skill, such as shooting, is first learned. As a novice shooter, you must think about your grip, the extension of your arms, and the proper alignment of sights. If you practice the shooting action enough (generally, several thousand times), these reflective activities can become reflexive. The action becomes automatic enough that system 2 is no longer needed to govern it. System 1 is able to perform the action automatically. You generally do not need to think (use system 2) to walk, for example. Once you train a skill to the point where it is a system 1 program, it is generally resistant to the negative effects of stress because it does not require system 2 monitoring (Staal 2004).

■ ***Use system 2 to develop scripts.*** Finally, you can use system 2 when you are not under stress to think about what you should do in a stressful situation. It is possible to think through likely scenarios and the appropriate responses to those scenarios to prepare action scripts. When under stress, you can then access these preprepared scripts.

While not as fast as performing an action that is programmed into system 1, you can execute these action plans faster than you can develop and execute an unplanned action. The plan that you have thought through beforehand is also likely to be of better quality than the one you come up with on the spot. This is particularly the case when your system 2 is starting to shut down due to the effects of stress.

The Decisive Moment

Ripley's (2008) final phase is the decisive moment. At this point, the potential victim has overcome denial and completed deliberation and must now act. Ripley describes this moment as "the sudden distillation of everything that has come before and it determines what, if anything, will come after" (2008, p. 143). This is the point at which the potential victim makes and executes a choice that may save or end his or her life.

A Case Study of the Response to a Life Threatening Disaster

In 2003, the band Great White was playing a show at a club called The Station. A small pyrotechnics display was part of the show. This display started a fire, which spread rapidly through the club and killed 100 people (Grosshandler et al. 2005).

Figure 8.1 is a diagram of the building. The band was playing in the area marked "raised platform." It has been estimated that 350 people were in attendance on that night. The majority of these people were probably in the area surrounding the band. The fire began at the location marked "ignition points." Eyewitnesses said that for several seconds after the fire started the club patrons did not react, suggesting that they were engaged in denial. After the patrons figured out that the building was on fire, panic ensued.

Figure 8.2 is a diagram of where people's bodies were located after the fire. As you can see, more than half of the people died near the main entrance of the building. You can also see that this entrance is quite narrow and probably became clogged with bodies shortly after the stampede to exit began. From the first diagram, you can see that there were three other available exits. The exit closest to the stage was probably not accessible for very long because it was close to the origin of the fire. The exit located in the kitchen may not have been visible

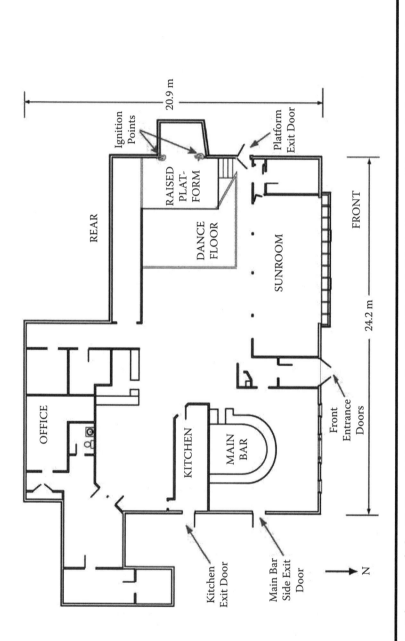

Figure 8.1   Diagram of The Station nightclub. (Grosshandler, W. et al. 2005. *Report of the technical investigation of The Station nightclub fire*. Washington, DC, Department of Commerce.)

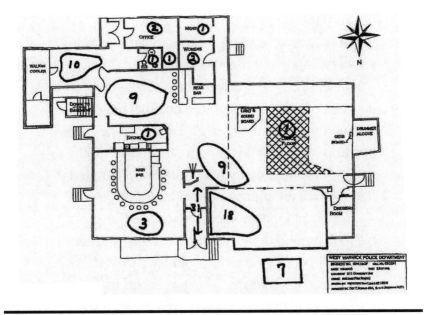

Figure 8.2   Diagram of the locations of the bodies. (Grosshandler, W. et al. 2005. *Report of the technical investigation of The Station nightclub fire.* **Washington, DC, Department of Commerce.)**

from the main area of the club, but the main bar side exit was visible from the main area of the club.

The obvious question is why the patrons packed into the impassable main entrance rather than using the main bar side exit. The material covered earlier in this chapter provides several possible reasons. The patrons were experiencing life-threatening stress. Their survival alarm systems were starting to go off. System 1 was taking over and system 2 was shutting down. Blood was being shunted to their large muscles to prepare for action. They were also probably experiencing tunnel vision and smoke was further limiting their ability to see. After they overcame several seconds of denial, they had to deliberate on a course of action. The high stress of the situation severely limited the patrons' abilities to do so. The patrons were probably only aware of the main entrance because this was the entrance they came in. System 1 was screaming at them to get out. Many could probably see that the main exit was not passable, but system 2 was not available to look actively for alternatives. In the decisive moment, the patrons made the correct decision to flee, but because of their limited information and inability to engage system 2, many of the patrons attempted to flee through an impassable exit and died.

How could the people have survived? A simple look around the location for alternative exits when the patrons came in could have placed that information in memory. Taking a second to think through using that exit could have created a script that could have been drawn upon to save lives when the fire started. Additionally, a few people making the choice to use an alternative exit could have provided enough social proof for other patrons to follow and have saved many lives.

We now turn to applying Ripley's (2008) steps to active shooter events.

Civilian Response to Active Shooter Events

As was mentioned earlier, the responses of potential victims (civilians) can have a dramatic impact on how many people are injured or killed in an active shooter event. Here we apply Ripley's (2008) disaster response arc specifically to active shooter events. We begin with denial and then move to deliberation and the decisive moment.

Denial

Overcoming denial in an active shooter event requires being aware of the signs of an active shooter event. The number one sign of an active shooter event is gunfire. This may sound obvious, but remember that your brain will try to describe unusual events as normal first (i.e., the normalcy bias). Most of us do not hear gunfire on a regular basis. Because of this, our brains will usually try to describe the gunfire as some more usual occurrence, like fireworks. This has happened in numerous active shooter events. People hear gunfire, but report that they thought it was firecrackers. Because firecrackers are not life threatening, the people at the scene delay taking action. As we have discussed before, this delay can cost lives.

Consider this: How many times have you heard firecrackers at your place of employment or school? For most of us, the answer to this question is zero. Given that this is the case and that gunfire poses a direct threat to your survival, does it not make sense to treat any sound that could be gunfire as gunfire and take immediate action? You might be embarrassed somewhat if it turns out that it was just firecrackers, but if the sound is actually gunfire, you may save your life and the lives of others.

To help overcome denial, we suggest a simple rule. If you hear something that could be gunfire, treat it as gunfire and take immediate action. In other words, skip denial and move straight to deliberation.

Deliberation and the Decisive Moment

Once you have made the determination that an active shooter event is occurring, you must consider your options and pick a course of action. As we discussed previously, your basic options are flight, fight, or freeze. Based on previous active shooter events, we are going to take freezing off the table as a viable action. The reason for this is simple. In case after case, people who either froze in place when the shooting started or attempted to play dead (another form of freezing) were attacked by the shooter anyway. The case study of Virginia Tech presented later will make this clear. This leaves flight or fight. At the Advanced Law Enforcement Rapid Response Training (ALERRT) Center, we teach two forms of flight (avoid and deny) and one form of fight (defend) to create a basic system that we call Avoid, Deny, Defend (ADD). This system is detailed next.

Avoid

The first response is to get away from the threat. If you can do so safely, leave the area in which the shooting is occurring to avoid the shooter. It is important that you move far enough away from the location of the event to be safe. In the case of a fire, this is often across the street. In an active shooter event, more distance (often a few blocks) is usually required to ensure that the shooter cannot shoot at you from inside the building and to ensure that if the shooter moves from his or her current location, you do not end up in the line of fire again.

Avoiding requires that you know the exit routes available to you. A few seconds spent thinking through the ways that you can get out of the locations that you are frequently in can save your life. Walking through the route when you are not under stress can provide you with a script that you can use when you are under stress. This is the reason that we do fire drills.

Deny

If it is unsafe to leave your current location to avoid the shooter, the next step is to take actions that will deny him access to your location. This is not hiding. It is doing what you can to prevent the shooter from getting into your location.

The simplest action—the one that has been extremely effective in the active shooter events that we have studied—is to lock the door to the room. In the attacks that have occurred in the United States, no shooter, to our knowledge, has breached a locked door. Locks that can be secured without the use of a key will be more useful in a crisis than locks that require one (putting a key into a lock is a fine motor activity that will likely be impaired in an active shooter attack). Obviously, locks to which most of the people in a location do not have a key are of little value.

Not all locations have doors that can be locked. If the door opens inward to the room, furniture can be used to barricade the door. Doorstops or other items can be wedged between the door and floor or frame to prevent it from opening.

Unfortunately, if the door opens outward (which is commonly required under modern building codes) and does not have a lock, denying access becomes much more difficult. Wedging or piling things on your side of the door will have little effect. It might be possible to use a rope to tie the door handle to something else, but this will be difficult to do under stress. It is probably easier to have locks installed or install a piece of hardware that can be used to keep the door closed in an emergency.

After the door is secure, you want to make the shooter think that no one is there. Turn off the lights to the room. Cover any windows that the shooter might see into the room through. Be quiet so that the shooter does not hear you.

Obviously, preplanning is important here as well. You should know options that you have to deny access and practice them to form scripts. If you do not have a reasonable way to secure the areas that you normally occupy, you should talk to your facility administrator and encourage her or him to improve the situation.

Denial is also a temporary phase because a determined attacker will eventually be able to gain access to your location. After you have provided yourself some immediate safety by securing your location, you should either begin looking for ways to avoid the shooter (such as going out a window) or prepare to defend yourself if the shooter gets into the room.

Defend

If you were unable to avoid the shooter or prevent him or her from gaining access to your location, there is only one option left. You must defend yourself. Admittedly, this is not a desirable situation as the shooter has a gun and you do not (see the section later on concealed carry if you do have a gun), but it is not hopeless. There are many active shooter events where the people on the scene were able to subdue the attacker and save their own lives. Next, we discuss some of the issues that surround protecting yourself.

Swarm the shooter. The point of defending yourself is not for it to be a fair fight. The purpose is to survive so that you get to go home. The shooter has superior firepower. You will probably have superior numbers. Use them. You want to plan with your group to swarm the shooter with as many people as possible when the shooter enters the room.

Positioning. You want to place yourself and others near, but not directly in front of, the door. You do not want to be directly in front of the door in case the shooter decides to fire through the door as he or she is trying to enter. You want to be close enough so that you can quickly attempt to get hold of the gun when the shooter enters. Generally, a few feet away is enough to keep you out of the line of fire, but close enough to get the shooter quickly. You also want to be in a position that requires the shooter to enter the room before you are seen. This positioning will usually be on the same wall on which the door is located. This is depicted in Figure 8.3. The Cs represent civilians in position to rush the shooter if he or she enters the room. The S represents where the shooter would enter through the door.

Actions. The task of the person nearest the door should be to get his or her hands on the shooter's gun as soon as

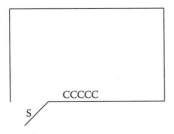

Figure 8.3 Positioning.

possible. Once his or her hands are on the gun, the person should attempt to get it pointed in a safe direction. This will usually be the floor or the ceiling, but it is also necessary to consider where the person is located. If there are floors above, the ground is probably safer. If there are floors below, the ceiling is probably safer.

The job of the rest of the group is to swarm the attacker and stop him or her. This is a deadly force situation. Most states recognize that you are allowed to use deadly force to protect yourself from the unlawful use of deadly force by another. You should check your local laws before using the techniques discussed here. This is not a fair fight. You want to stop the attacker as soon as possible. You can punch, kick, pull hair, bite, gouge, use improvised weapons, or do anything else necessary to stop the attacker.

What to expect. This will be an extremely violent encounter. The gun may go off. If it does, it will be extremely loud. If you are attempting to hold the gun when it goes off, it may cut your hands or get extremely hot. You may be shot. Unlike what happens on TV and the movies, being shot does not mean that you are dead. The fact that you are still conscious and aware after being shot means that there is a good chance you will survive. Keep fighting until the shooter is stopped no matter how injured you are.

Concealed handguns. If you are a concealed handgun carrier and you find yourself in one of these situations, there are some special considerations. First, we have placed this section under "Defend" because we believe that it is the appropriate place for it. The gun is your last line of defense to be used when you were unable to avoid the shooter or deny him access to your location. The last thing that you want to do in an active shooter event is to pull your gun out and go hunting for the shooter. If there are other concealed handgun carriers in the attack location, they may shoot you. If the police show up and you are running around with a gun, they will probably shoot you. Remember that no one knows who you are. The responders are looking for someone with a gun and you match that description.

If you are able to avoid the shooter, you should leave like everyone else. If you attempt to deny access to a room, the place for the handgun is in defending yourself if the shooter comes into the room. Make sure that you have a clear line of fire to the door. Know your backdrop. Where will your bullets go if you miss? This last thing you want to have happen is that you kill innocent people while trying to stop the shooter.

As important as being ready to defend yourself is that you also need to communicate your position and description to emergency personnel as soon as possible. If you are with a group, have someone else call 911 and give your location and description. If you are by yourself, you will need to call 911.

If the police enter the room that you are in, you must put the gun down and show your hands as quickly as possible. Do not try to tell them who you are. Get the gun out of your hands or they may shoot you.

Communication. Regardless of the particular strategy you use to protect yourself, you generally want to communicate with emergency personnel as soon as it is reasonably safe to do so. If you avoided the shooter and are at safe location, you can now call 911 and give them any information that you have on the shooter and the event. If you denied access to your location and are still in a secured room, you should also call 911 to communicate your location, the number of people with you, and any information you have about the attack. If you defended yourself and the attacker has been stopped, emergency personnel need to know this as well.

What to Expect When the Police Arrive

After the first call of an active shooter goes out, the police will be coming as quickly as they can. Next we detail what you should expect from them when they get on scene

- ▪ ***Agencies.*** Police from every agency in the vicinity can be expected to respond. You will see a variety of different uniforms and probably some plainclothes officers. You will see officers from a variety of organizations, some of which you will have never heard.
- ▪ ***Priority of work.*** The first priority for the responding officers is to stop the killing. Next, they will help the wounded, and, finally, they will escort people from the building. This means that until the officers are certain that the shooter is stopped, the responding officers will not stop to help you. It is not because they do not care. It is because they must prioritize their work to protect others and themselves. The officers must make sure that the shooter is stopped before helping anyone else. Let the officers do their jobs. Give them information about the shooter if you have it, but do not attempt to get them to stop and help you.
- ▪ ***How to behave.*** This event will be extremely tense for the responding officers. They will be experiencing all the symptoms of stress that we discussed earlier. Also remember that wherever they are responding to the shooting, you probably fit the profile of the shooter. If it is a school, the most likely suspect will be a student. If it is a workplace, the most likely shooter will be an employee or ex-employee. Make the officers' jobs as easy as possible. Show the palms of your open hands. Do not move. If you

have to move, move slowly. Comply immediately with any commands that you are given. You may be handcuffed while the situation is sorted out. Do not argue with the officers. The time for complaints and arguments is after the situation has been resolved.

■ ***Aftermath.*** Following an active shooter attack, you should be prepared for several things. First, you will lose access to the facility for a substantial period of time while the investigation is conducted. At a minimum, this will be hours, but more likely it will be days. Second, you should expect there to be substantial mental trauma. People will exhibit signs of shock and, potentially, posttraumatic stress disorder (PTSD) in the longer term. Nightmares will be common, and many of the survivors may experience guilt at having survived when others did not. These are all normal and predictable responses. It is important that organizations have a critical incident stress management plan in place to help their people deal with these issues. If you are in one of these events, you should take advantage of whatever services are offered, and if they are not you should seek out help.

A Case Study of Civilian Response to an Active Shooter Event

This section discusses the civilian response to the Virginia Tech shooter in April of 2007. The Virginia Tech attack provides an interesting case study because the shooter attacked (or attempted to attack) five classrooms in Norris Hall. Each of these rooms responded differently and each suffered different percentages of killed and wounded.

The attack began in room 206 (Giduck 2011; Virginia Tech Review Panel 2007). The shooter stepped into the door and began firing at the students. He then walked down the aisle shooting students. Two students from 204 looked into the hallway to see what was happening. They decided to make a run for it. One was shot, but both survived. Professor Librescu, in room 204, saw and heard the shooting, held the door closed with his body, and ordered his students to jump out of the window.

The shooter then attacked room 207 in much the same way that he attacked 206. The professor in 211 saw the shooter shooting at people in the hallway. He retreated into the class and they started trying to barricade the door with lightweight student's desks. A student in 211 called 911.

The shooter moved to 211 and pushed his way through the desks. Air Force Cadet Matthew LaPorte charged the shooter by himself. He was shot several times and killed before he reached the shooter. The shooter then opened fire on the rest of classroom.

The shooter then left 211 and attacked 206 again. The people in 206 were either dead or playing dead. The shooter walked down the aisles shooting people.

The shooter left 206 and attempted to attack 207 again. Four students (two that had been shot in the first attack and two others) held the door closed with their hands and feet while keeping their bodies out of the way. The shooter attempted to push the door open and when he could not, he fired through the door. His shots did not hit anyone.

The shooter moved away from 207 to 205. The students in 205 had pushed a large teacher's desk against the door and were holding it there. The shooter fired through the door, but did not hit anyone and failed to gain access to the room.

Next, the shooter moved to 204 and attempted to gain entry. This is the room where Professor Librescu was barricading the door with his body.

The shooter fired through the door hitting Librescu, muscled his way in, and shot Librescu in the head. Most of the students had made it out of the windows by this time. The shooter shot those who had not escaped.

After that, the shooter attacked 206 again and then attacked 211 again. In each of these rooms he moved up and down the aisles shooting people who were either dead or pretending to be dead. The shooter killed himself in 211. It is believed that he killed himself because he heard the police officers ascending the stairwell to the second floor.

Figure 8.4 presents the number of people shot and killed in each of the rooms. In room 206 where the potential victims took no defensive actions other than freezing, 92% of the people were shot and more than three-quarters of them died. In room 211, where the potential victims attempted unsuccessfully to barricade the door and Cadet LaPorte attempted to attack the shooter, everyone was shot and about two-thirds were killed. In room 207, no initial defensive action was taken, but the

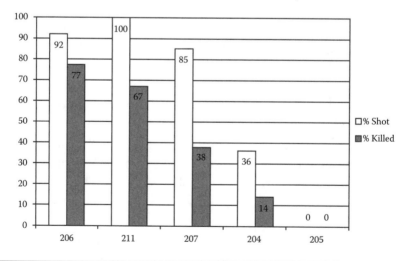

Figure 8.4 Number of people shot and killed at Virginia Tech.

potential victims successfully barricaded the door to prevent the shooter from reentering. Here, 85% of the people were shot and 38% died. Room 204 performed a denial and then attempted to avoid the shooter. While the denial was ultimately unsuccessful, it provided most of the students with time to escape. In this room, 36% of the occupants were shot and 14% were killed. Room 205 successfully denied the shooter access to the room. The shooter fired through the door, but no one was hit or killed.

The data show a clear pattern that those who took some form of defensive action at Virginia Tech fared much better than those who did not. Freezing or playing dead were not good options.

Also consider the ASE resolution flow chart in Chapter 3 (p. 62). About half of all active shooter events between 2000 and 2010 ended before the police arrived. In 39% of the attacks that were stopped before the police arrived, the victims took action to stop the shooter themselves either by physically subduing the attacker (81%) or by shooting him with their own personal weapons (19%). These data clearly show that it is possible to defend yourself successfully in these events even if you are unarmed.

In the other 61% of ASEs that stopped before the police arrived, the shooter either left the scene (16%) or killed himself or herself (84%). While we cannot know for certain why the shooter chose suicide or to leave before the police arrived, it seems, in many cases, that the shooter killed himself or herself or left when there were no more easily accessible victims to attack. In other words, it appears that the potential victims in many of these cases successfully avoided or denied the shooter access to their locations and the shooter then either killed himself or herself or left.

Taken together, the Virginia Tech case study and our data on ASEs from 2000 to 2010 create a clear picture. You are not helpless during these events! What you do matters! Using the avoid, deny, defend (ADD) framework, you can save not only your own life, but also the lives of others!

Policy

We conclude this section by offering some insights on developing policies for response to active shooter events and giving a very basic policy example. Perhaps the most important issue that we have seen in policies is that they are written in a one-response-fits-all-situations manner. We have seen schools, for example, that have policies that state that in the event of an active shooter, the school is to go into lockdown (a form of denial). This may be effective if the shooting starts in some other area of the building and the faculty and staff are able to lock their doors to deny access to their area of the building, but what if the shooting starts in a classroom or happens in a crowded lunchroom? What if the shooter has detonated explosives in the building that have either caused a fire or damaged the structural integrity of the building? Clearly, in these cases, people need options other than lockdown.

The second issue that we have seen is that policies are written so specifically that they attempt to give specific guidance for every possible active shooter situation. These policies tend to be extremely long. This would suggest that people will not read or be able to remember what the policy says (particularly in a crisis situation when system 2 is impaired). Additionally, as you have seen from the earlier reviews of active shooter cases, there is substantial variability in how these attacks are conducted. It is simply not possible to write a policy that will address every possibility.

We recommend that policies be written to be general, easy to understand, and simple to remember. It is also necessary to provide training to employees, faculty, and staff on what the policy means and what is expected if an active shooter event does occur. An example of such a policy, targeted at a business, is presented here. Obviously, this policy would have to be modified to fit the particular needs of a specific facility and reviewed by legal counsel before it is put into use.

Example Policy

- Our organization places the highest priority on the preservation of the lives of our employees and customers. If an active shooter event should occur, our employees shall use the "avoid, deny, defend" model.
- If it is safe for them to do so, employees should exit the facility immediately to AVOID the shooter(s).
- If employees are unable to exit the facility safely, they should lock themselves in their current location and barricade the door to DENY the shooter(s) access.
- In the event that employees are unable to utilize the AVOID and DENY strategies successfully, they should DEFEND themselves using whatever means are available.
- Regardless of the option(s) utilized, employees shall call emergency services (911) as soon as it is safe to do so.
- In the event of an active shooter incident, all employees will be required to undergo mandatory mental health counseling.

References

Artwohl, A., and L. W. Christensen. 1997. *Deadly force encounters: What cops need to know to mentally and physically prepare for and survive a gunfight.* Boulder, CO: Paladin Press.

Cialdini, R. B. 2008. *Influence: Science and practices.* 5th ed. Upper Saddle River, NJ: Prentice Hall.

Giduck, J. 2011. *Shooter down: The dramatic, untold story of the police response to the Virginia Tech massacre.* Golden, CO: Archangel Group, Ltd.

Grosshandler, W., N. Bryner, D. Madrzykowski, and K. Kuntz. 2005. *Report of the technical investigation of the station night club fire.* Washington, DC: Department of Commerce.

Grossman, D. 2008. *On combat: The psychology and physiology of deadly conflict in war and peace,* 3rd ed. Millstadt, IL: Warrior Science Publications.

Kahneman, D. 2011. *Thinking, fast and slow.* New York: Farrar, Straus, & Giroux.

Klinger, D. A., and R. K. Brunson. 2009. Police officers' perceptual distortions during lethal force situations: Informing the reasonableness standard. *Criminology & Public Policy* 8:117–140.

LeDoux, J. 1996. *The emotional brain: The mysterious underpinnings of emotional life.* New York: Simon & Schuster.

National Institute of Standards and Technology. 2005. *Final report on the collapse of the World Trade Center towers.* Department of Commerce.

Pinizzotto, A. J., E. F. Davis, and C. E. Miller. 2004. *Violent encounters: A study of felonious assaults on our nation's law enforcement officers.* Washington, DC: Department of Justice.

Ripley, A. 2008. *The unthinkable: Who survives when disaster strikes and why.* New York: Three Rivers Press.

Saunders, T., J. E. Driskell, J. H. Johnston, and E. Salas. 1996. The effect of stress inoculation training on anxiety and performance. *Journal of Occupational Health Psychology* 1:170–186.

Staal, M. A. 2004. Stress, cognition, and human performance: A literature review and conceptual framework. Moffett Field, CA: NASA.

Virginia Tech Review Panel. 2007. *Mass shootings at Virginia Tech.*

Appendix

Brief Summaries of Active Shooter Events from 2000 to 2010

Prepared by M. Hunter Martaindale

December 14, 2010

A 56-year-old male armed with a 9mm pistol attacked a school board meeting in Panama City, Florida. He entered the meeting and told everyone except the school board members to leave. A security guard was on scene at the time of the shooting. Upon exchanging gunfire with the security guard, the shooter killed himself. None of the intended victims were shot. (Sources: agency report and news articles)

October 14, 2010

An unknown male attacked a sanitation department maintenance yard in Washington, DC. The shooter randomly started shooting and then left the scene before police arrived. Two people were shot and one died. (Sources: supplemental homicide reports [SHRs] and news articles)

October 9, 2010

A 41-year-old male armed with a .357 magnum pistol attacked a grade school in Carlsbad, California. The shooter jumped the fence surrounding the school and opened fire at a group of students. Two construction workers tackled the shooter before police arrived. Two people were shot, but none were killed. (Sources: news articles)

October 5, 2010

A 24-year-old male armed with a .38-caliber pistol randomly shot at people as he drove around Gainesville, Florida. Police arrived at the first scene within 1 minute; however, the shooter was mobile. He committed suicide 13 minutes after the shooting started. Five people were shot and two were killed. (Sources: agency report and news articles)

September 27, 2010

A 26-year-old male armed with a pistol attacked the Americold Logistics plant in Crete, Nebraska. He was an employee of the factory and opened fire in the employee break room. The shooter walked outside the factory and killed himself before police could arrive on scene. Three people were shot, but none were killed. (Sources: news articles)

September 20, 2010

A 63-year-old male armed with a pistol attacked a convenience store located on Ft. Bliss in El Paso, Texas. He entered the front door of the store and opened fire. Police arrived on scene in 3 minutes and shot the attacker. Two people were shot and one died. (Sources: news articles)

September 10, 2010

A 43-year-old female armed with a .357 magnum pistol attacked the Kraft Foods factory in Philadelphia, Pennsylvania. She had been suspended from her job and returned later to start shooting. Police were on scene in 6 minutes and immediately were shot at. The attacker was taken into custody by the SWAT team approximately 40 minutes later. The shooter did not kill anybody after law enforcement arrived on scene. Three people were shot and two died. (Sources: agency report, SHRs, and news articles)

August 3, 2010

A 34-year-old male armed with a pistol attacked the beer distribution center he worked at in Manchester, Connecticut. After being caught stealing beer, he was offered an opportunity to quit rather than be fired. He then opened fire. Police were on scene in 3 minutes and the shooter committed suicide after their arrival. Ten people were shot and eight died. (Sources: agency report, SHRs, and news articles)

July 12, 2010

A 37-year-old male armed with a pistol attacked the Emcore Corporation building in Albuquerque, New Mexico. He arrived at the location, confronted his girlfriend, and then opened fire throughout the building. Police were on scene within a minute and formed an active shooter response team before entering 2 minutes later. The shooter went further into the building and killed himself. Nine people were shot and two died. (Sources: agency report, SHRs, and news articles)

June 9, 2010

A 38-year-old male armed with a .45-caliber pistol attacked the Yoyito Café in Hialeah, Florida. Even though an employee of the café attempted to lock the door, the shooter was able to enter the building and open fire. Police were on scene in 5 minutes, but the shooter had already killed himself. Six people were shot and three died. (Sources: agency report and news articles)

May 27, 2010

A 79-year-old male armed with a .38-caliber pistol attacked an AT&T Wireless store in New York Mills, New York. He entered the store after receiving a written complaint from the store for an incident a couple of days prior and opened fire. He had plans to kill the six employees that had reported him. An off-duty police officer shot and killed the shooter. One person was shot and none died. (Sources: news articles)

May 18, 2010

A 50-year-old male armed with a pistol attacked the Boulder Stove & Flooring store in Boulder, Colorado. He was an employee of the store and opened fire in the back office. Police arrived on scene in 4 minutes, but the shooter had already killed himself. Two people were shot and both died. (Sources: agency report, SHRs, and news articles)

May 10, 2010

A 17-year-old male armed with a pistol attacked an outdoor carnival in Bloomfield, New Jersey. He was running through a crowd indiscriminately shooting. A police officer who was working the carnival was in the area of the shooting. He shot and killed the shooter. One person was shot and none died. (Sources: news articles)

March 30, 2010

A 44-year-old female armed with a pistol attacked the Publix Super Market in Tarpon Springs, Florida. She had been terminated after making threats to a co-worker and returned later with the weapon. After killing her supervisor in front of the store, she entered the building and continued shooting. An officer arrived on scene shortly after and confronted the shooter in the store. As she fired at the shooter he shot and killed her. One person was shot and killed. (Sources: news articles)

March 9, 2010

A 50-year-old male armed with both a .45-caliber and 9mm pistol attacked The Ohio State University maintenance building in Columbus, Ohio. The shooter had been terminated for falsifying his job application. He opened fire on his supervisors and then killed himself. Police arrived on scene 2 minutes after the initial report and after he had committed suicide. Two people were shot; one was killed. (Sources: agency report, SHRs, news articles)

March 2, 2010

A 19-year-old male armed with a semiautomatic rifle attacked the Farm King store in Macomb, Illinois. The shooter entered the building and opened fire. Police arrived on scene 2 minutes after the initial report and received fire from the shooter. The shooter hid in the store with several hostages for over 4 hours until he killed himself. Nobody was shot in the incident. (Sources: agency report and news articles)

February 23, 2010

A 32-year-old male armed with a .30-06 hunting rifle attacked the Deer Creek Middle School in Littleton, Colorado. The shooter walked up to a group of students and opened fire. A nearby teacher subdued the shooter while he was attempting to load another round. Police arrived on scene within minutes, but the shooter was already subdued. Two people were shot and none were killed. (Sources: news articles)

February 12, 2010

A 44-year-old female attacked a faculty meeting with a 9mm pistol at the University of Alabama in Huntsville, Alabama. The shooter sat in on a faculty meeting for 30 minutes before standing up and opening fire. She walked out the front door and was apprehended by police officers 3 minutes later. Six people were shot and three were killed. (Sources: news articles)

February 10, 2010

A 48-year-old male armed with a pistol attacked the Inskip Elementary School in Knoxville, Tennessee. The shooter was an employee of the school and opened fire on members of the administration. He fled the scene only to be stuck in a construction roadblock. Police apprehended him 14 minutes after the initial report. Two people were shot and none were killed. (Sources: agency report, news articles)

January 19, 2010

A 55-year-old shooter armed with a pistol attacked a home business in Brooksville, Florida, before going mobile. After opening fire on several unrelated victims, the shooter fled and got into a shootout with law enforcement. He shot and killed one police officer before being shot. Six people were shot and four were killed. (Sources: agency report and news articles)

January 8, 2010

A 51-year-old male armed with multiple weapons (i.e., 7.62 assault rifle, two pistols, and a 12-gauge shotgun) attacked the ABB plant in St. Louis, Missouri. The shooter, a disgruntled employee, opened fire in the parking lot before moving into the plant. Police were on scene 4 minutes after being notified, but the shooter killed himself before they arrived. Eight people were shot, three of whom died. (Sources: SHRs and news articles)

December 23, 2009

A 53-year-old male armed with a pistol attacked Grady Crawford Construction in Baton Rouge, Louisiana. The shooter arrived on site and immediately opened fire. Police were on scene in 4 minutes; however, co-workers had already subdued the shooter. Three people were shot, two of whom died. (Sources: agency report, SHRs, news articles)

November 30, 2009

A 37-year-old male armed with a pistol attacked four police officers at the Forza Coffee Shop in Tacoma, Washington. The shooter walked into the coffee shop and instantly shot the four officers. He then fled the scene and was captured a few days later after an exhaustive manhunt. Four people were shot, all of whom died. (Sources: SHRs and news articles)

November 17, 2009

A 24-year-old male armed with a 9mm pistol attacked a crowd of people at Hudson Docket in Valdosta, Georgia. The shooter got into an altercation and opened fire indiscriminately into the crowd. Police were on scene in 6 minutes; however, the shooter had fled the scene. He was apprehended the next day. One of the 12 people shot died. (Sources: agency report, SHRs, news articles)

November 7, 2009

A 39-year-old male armed with both a 5.7 pistol and a .357 revolver attacked Fort Hood in Fort Hood, Texas. The shooter entered the Soldier Readiness Processing Center and opened fire. Police were on scene in 3 minutes as the shooter transitioned outside. The shooter exchanged gunfire with the first responders and hit one. The second officer shot him and secured his weapons. Of the 42 people shot, 13 died. (Sources: agency report and news articles)

November 6, 2009

A 40-year-old male armed with a pistol attacked Reynolds Smith & Hall located in Orlando, Florida. The shooter was an ex-employee. Upon entering the building he opened fire. He left the scene before police arrived. He surrendered to law enforcement a little over 2 hours later. Six people were shot, one of whom died. (Sources: news articles)

September 11, 2009

A 33-year-old male armed with a pistol attacked multiple locations (i.e., outside a school and a gravel quarry) in Owosso, Michigan. The shooter, after dropping off his children, first shot a protestor in the street in front of the school and then drove to the gravel quarry to continue shooting. He surrendered to law enforcement 2.5 hours after he started. Two people were shot and killed. (Sources: agency report, SHRs, news articles)

August 5, 2009

A 48-year-old male armed with two pistols attacked the LA Fitness center in Collier Township, Pennsylvania. The shooter walked into the gym with a gym bag containing both pistols and opened fire. Police arrived on scene in 5 minutes, but the shooter had already killed himself. Twelve people were shot, three of whom died. (Sources: SHRs and news articles)

June 10, 2009

An 88-year-old male armed with a .22-caliber rifle attacked the Holocaust Museum in Washington, DC. The shooter walked up to the entrance and shot the security guard attending the front door. Two additional security guards opened fire and shot the shooter. One person was shot and killed. (Sources: SHRs and news articles)

June 1, 2009

A 24-year-old male armed with multiple weapons (i.e., AK–47, .22-caliber rifle, and a handgun) attacked the United States Army Recruiting Center in Little Rock, Arkansas. The shooter drove up and opened fire on soldiers standing outside the recruiting center. The shooter fled the scene and was apprehended a couple of minutes later without incident. Two people were shot, one of whom died. (Sources: news articles)

May 18, 2009

A 15-year-old male armed with a .25-caliber pistol attacked the Larose-Cut Off Middle School in Cut Off, Louisiana. The shooter entered a classroom and discharged the weapon. He then committed suicide before law enforcement arrived. Nobody was shot. (Sources: news articles)

April 26, 2009

An 18-year-old male armed with a 9mm pistol attacked Harkness Hall at Hampton University in Hampton, Virginia. The shooter entered the dorm behind a deliveryman and opened fire. Police were on scene 2 minutes later, but the shooter had committed suicide before their arrival. Two people were shot, but none were killed. (Sources: agency report and news articles)

April 9, 2009

A 69-year-old male armed with a .32-caliber revolver attacked residents of the Kkottongnae Retreat Camp in Temecula, California. The shooter walked from building to building and opened fire. In the second building the citizens fought back and subdued the shooter before police arrived. Police arrived on scene 10 minutes after the initial report and formed active shooter teams to clear every building. Four people were shot, one of whom was killed. (Sources: agency report, SHRs, news articles)

April 4, 2009

A 42-year-old male armed with both a .45-caliber and a 9mm pistol attacked the American Civic Association in Binghamton, New York. The shooter blocked the back door with his vehicle and then entered the front door. Upon entering the building, he opened fire. Police arrived on scene in 2 minutes, but the shooter had already committed suicide. Of the 16 people shot, 13 were killed. (Sources: agency report, SHRs, news articles)

March 29, 2009

A 45-year-old male armed with a pistol attacked the Pinelake Health & Rehabilitation Center in Carthage, North Carolina. The shooter started indiscriminately shooting residents. A Carthage police officer was at the location and exchanged gunfire with the shooter. The police officer was wounded, but he was able to wound the shooter as well. Eight people were shot, six of whom were killed. (Sources: agency report, SHRs, news articles)

March 11, 2009

A 28-year-old male armed with an assault rifle attacked multiple locations across two counties in southeast Alabama. The shooter attacked three locations starting near his home and then shot at random individuals as he drove. He ended the event at the Reliable Metal Products plant in Geneva, Alabama. After exchanging gunfire with responding police, the shooter committed suicide. In total, the event lasted 47 minutes. Of the 11 people shot, 10 were killed. (Sources: news articles)

January 24, 2009

A 24-year-old male armed with a 9mm pistol attacked The Zone, an nightclub for underage patrons in Portland, Oregon. The shooter drove to the downtown club and opened fire on a random crowd and then immediately committed suicide well before police could arrive on scene. Nine people were shot, two of whom were killed. (Sources: SHRs and news articles)

September 2, 2008

A 28-year-old armed with an assault rifle attacked multiple locations along I-5 in Skagit County in Washington. The shooter originally opened fire at a police officer at his home. At this time, he proceeded to drive down I-5, randomly shooting commuters and another police officer. The event ended 40 minutes later when he drove to a police station and surrendered. Eight people were shot, six of whom were killed. (Sources: agency report, SHRs, news articles)

July 28, 2008

A 58-year-old male armed with a 12-gauge shotgun attacked the Tennessee Valley Unitarian Universalist Church in Knoxville, Tennessee. The shooter entered the church during a youth production and opened fire on the first pew. As soon as the shooting started, three members subdued the shooter. Police were on scene in 3 minutes, but the citizens had already subdued the shooter. Nine people were shot, two of whom were killed. (Sources: agency reports, SHRs, news articles)

May 29, 2008

A 30-year-old male armed with a pistol attacked the Players Bar and Grill in Winnemucca, Nevada. The shooter entered the front door and indiscriminately opened fire, reloaded, and continued firing. A citizen with a concealed handgun license opened fire on the shooter before law enforcement arrived. Four people were shot, two of whom were killed. (Sources: SHRs and news articles)

February 14, 2008

A 27-year-old male armed with a shotgun attacked the Cole Hall Auditorium on the campus of Northern Illinois University in DeKalb, Illinois. The shooter walked into the classroom and started indiscriminately shooting students before committing suicide. Campus police were on scene within a minute of the initial report, but the shooter had already committed suicide. Twenty-six people were shot, five of whom were killed. (Sources: agency report and news articles)

February 8, 2008

A 23-year-old female armed with a pistol attacked the Louisiana Technical College located in Baton Rouge, Louisiana. The shooter walked into a classroom, pulled a pistol from her purse, and opened fire. Police were on scene in 4 minutes, but the shooter had already committed suicide. Two people were shot and killed. (Sources: SHRs and news articles)

February 7, 2008

A 52-year-old male armed with both a .44 magnum revolver and a .40-caliber pistol attacked the City Hall Building in Kirkwood, Missouri. Outside the building, the shooter shot a police officer and took his weapon before entering. Once inside City Hall, he shot another police officer and opened fire on the rest of the people. The police department was located across the street and the gunfire was audible. Two officers arrived on scene minutes after the shooting started. The officers shot the shooter while exchanging gunfire with him. Seven people were shot, five of whom were killed. (Sources: SHRs and news articles)

December 9, 2007

A 24-year-old male armed with three weapons (.223 assault rifle, .40-caliber pistol, and a 9mm pistol) attacked two churches located at Arvada and Colorado Springs, Colorado. At 12:30 a.m. the shooter attacked the Arvada location. After being denied entry he opened fire and fled the scene. Around 1 a.m. he arrived at the Colorado Springs location. Upon entering the foyer he opened fire before being shot by an armed security guard, killing him. Nine people were shot, four of whom were killed. (Sources: agency report, SHRs, news articles)

December 5, 2007

A 19-year-old male armed with an AK-47 variant assault rifle attacked the Westroads Mall's Von Maur store in Omaha, Nebraska. The shooter exited the elevator on the third floor and opened fire. Police were on scene 6 minutes after being contacted, but the shooter had already killed himself. Thirteen people were shot, eight of whom were killed. (Sources: agency report and news articles)

October 10, 2007

A 14-year-old male armed with both .38- and .22-caliber pistols attacked the SuccessTech Academy located in Cleveland, Ohio. The shooter walked up two flights of stairs before opening fire in the crowded hallway of the third floor. The shooter walked up to the fourth floor and continued shooting before killing himself prior to police arrival. Four people were shot, none of whom were killed. (Sources: news articles)

August 8, 2007

A 43-year-old male armed with a pistol attacked Liberty Transportation located in Millbury, Ohio. The shooter was being terminated for poor work performance when he opened fire in the office. Police were on scene in 5 minutes, but the shooter had already fled the scene. He was arrested about 2 hours later without incident. Two people were shot; both were killed. (Sources: agency report and news articles)

May 1, 2007

A 51-year-old male armed with an assault rifle attacked a Target store in Kansas City, Missouri. The shooter was pulled over, at which time he shot the police officer. He then drove to the shopping center and opened fire in the parking lot while moving into the store. Police arrived and entered the store, shooting and killing him 16 minutes after he was pulled over and the event started. Ten people were shot, two of whom were killed. (Sources: SHRs and news articles)

April 16, 2007

A 23-year-old male armed with a 9mm and a .22-caliber pistol attacked Virginia Polytech in Blacksburg, Virginia. Two and a half hours after attacking two individuals in a dorm, the shooter chained the doors shut in an academic building. He then systematically attacked the students and faculty inside the building. Law enforcement, already on campus for the first attack, were on scene in 3 minutes. Five minutes passed until the officers were able to breach the building. While using a shotgun to enter the building, the shooter committed suicide. Of the 49 people shot, 32 were killed. (Sources: agency report, SHRs, news articles)

February 12, 2007

A 44-year-old male armed with an AK-47 and a .40-caliber handgun attacked the Zigzag Net Inc. office located in Philadelphia, Pennsylvania. While at a board meeting dealing with a financial dispute, the shooter opened fire. Police were on scene 2 minutes after being notified. The shooter opened fire at the first responders and then committed suicide. Four people were shot, three of whom were killed. (Sources: agency report, SHRs, news articles)

February 12, 2007

An 18-year-old male armed with a shotgun attacked the Trolley Square Mall located in Salt Lake City, Utah. The shooter entered the mall and started indiscriminately shooting. Police were on scene in 2 minutes and formed an active shooter response team. Upon entering the mall, the police shot and killed the shooter. Nine people were shot, five of whom were killed. (Sources: agency report, SHRs, news articles)

October 10, 2006

A 13-year-old male armed with an AK-47 attacked Joplin Memorial Middle School located in Joplin, Missouri. The shooter entered a classroom and opened fire. His rifle jammed after one shot. He left the scene and was followed by security that directed law enforcement to his location. He was arrested without incident 9 minutes later. Nobody was shot. (Sources: agency report and news articles)

October 2, 2006

A 32-year-old male armed with three weapons (assault rifle, shotgun, pistol) attacked the West Nickel Mines School located in Bart Township, Pennsylvania. The shooter entered the school building and ordered the males and adults out and boarded the doors. Police were on scene 6 minutes after initial notification. The shooter opened fire in the schoolhouse approximately 20 minutes after police arrived. The shooter committed suicide before police could enter the building. Ten people were shot, five of whom were killed. (Sources: SHRs and news articles)

September 29, 2006

A 15-year-old male armed with both a shotgun and .22-caliber pistol attacked Weston High School located in Cazenovia, Wisconsin. The shooter entered the school and opened fire. As soon as the shooting started, employees of the school subdued the shooter until police arrived. One person was shot and killed. (Sources: SHR and news articles)

August 30, 2006

A 19-year-old male armed with a rifle attacked Orange High School located in Hillsborough, North Carolina. The shooter, after killing his father at home early in the morning, drove to the school where he opened fire from his vehicle. Police were on scene in 2 minutes and took the shooter into custody without incident. Two students were injured; none were killed. (Sources: news articles)

August 26, 2006

A 26-year-old male armed with a pistol attacked multiple locations, including Essex Elementary School, in Essex, Vermont. After opening fire at a home, the shooter attacked Essex Elementary School. The shooter fled the school and moved to a third location where he opened fire again. He shot himself before police arrived. Including all three locations, four people were shot, three of whom were killed. (Sources: agency report, SHRs, news articles)

March 14, 2006

A 14-year-old male armed with a .38-caliber pistol attacked Pine Middle School located in Reno, Nevada. The shooter opened fire outside the school cafeteria. A teacher coaxed him to stop shooting and then subdued him with a "bear-hug" until police arrived on scene. Two people were shot; neither was killed. (Sources: news articles)

November 22, 2005

A 20-year-old male armed with both an assault rifle and pistol attacked the Tacoma Mall located in Tacoma, Washington. The shooter opened fire indiscriminately as he entered the mall. The shooter ended up taking four victims hostage in a record store. After approximately 3 hours, the local SWAT team subdued the shooter without incident. Six people were shot, none of whom were killed. (Sources: news articles)

November 22, 2005

An unknown male armed with an "assault-style" weapon attacked multiple locations in North Augusta, South Carolina. After opening fire at a Burger King, the shooter ran to a Huddle House Restaurant, where he continued shooting. The shooter then fled the scene and was never identified. Three people were shot, one of whom was killed. (Sources: agency report, SHRs, news articles)

October 8, 2005

A 15-year-old male armed with a .22-caliber pistol attacked Campbell County Comprehensive High School in Jacksboro,

Tennessee. The shooter hid the pistol under a napkin and opened fire at administrators as they walked through a common area. Fellow administrators and students subdued the shooter until police arrived. Three people were shot; one was killed. (Sources: news articles)

October 7, 2005

An unknown male armed with a pistol attacked two unrelated individuals in public locations in Philadelphia, Pennsylvania. The shooter shot one bystander and then drove to a separate parking lot where he shot another bystander. An off-duty police officer saw the shooting and opened fire. The officer wounded the shooter, who then killed himself. Two people were shot; both were killed. (Sources: agency report, SHRs, news articles)

August 9, 2005

A 35-year-old male armed with a pistol attacked both a car dealership and bystanders at a separate location in Colton, California. The shooter arrived at the car dealership with a grievance. He then opened fire and fled the scene. Twenty minutes after fleeing the car dealership, he opened fire on unrelated bystanders at an apartment complex and fled again. The next day a police officer recognized the shooter and exchanged fire, shooting the shooter. Six people were shot at both locations, three of whom were killed. (Sources: SHRs and news articles)

May 21, 2005

A 16-year-old male armed with multiple weapons (shotgun, duty pistol, and a .22-caliber pistol) along with a bulletproof vest attacked Red Lake High School located in Red Lake, Minnesota. The shooter first shot his grandfather and stole his shotgun, duty pistol, and bulletproof vest before driving to the high school. Upon entering the school, the shooter "roamed through the school, firing randomly." Police were on scene within 5 minutes. After exchanging gunfire with four police officers, the shooter retreated and killed himself. Eleven people were shot, nine of whom were killed. (Sources: agency report and news articles)

April 12, 2005

A 44-year-old male armed with a 9mm pistol attacked the Living Church of God at the Sheraton Hotel conference room located in Brookfield, Wisconsin. The shooter entered the church and began indiscriminately shooting members. Police were on scene in 3 minutes and entered the scene 2 minutes later. However, the shooter had already killed himself before their arrival. Eleven people were shot; seven of whom were killed. (Sources: agency report and news articles)

February 13, 2005

A 24-year-old male armed with an AK-47 variant attacked the Hudson Valley Mall near Kingston, New York. The shooter opened fire inside a Best Buy store before moving further into the mall. He continued shooting until he ran out of ammunition, at which point two mall workers subdued him until police arrived. Two people were shot; neither was killed. (Sources: agency report and news articles)

November 18, 2004

A 25-year-old male armed with a .40-caliber pistol attacked a Radio Shack in St. Petersburg, Florida. The shooter entered the front door and started shooting without warning. He killed himself before police were even notified of the shooting. Three people were shot; two of whom were killed. (Sources: news articles)

February 9, 2004

A 16-year-old male armed with a 12-gauge shotgun attacked Columbia High School located in East Greenbush, New York. The shooter opened fire while walking through the school. Administrators confronted the shooter, wrestled the shotgun away, and subdued him before law enforcement arrived on scene. One person was shot and survived. (Sources: agency report and news articles)

September 24, 2003

A 15-year-old male armed with a .22-caliber pistol attacked Rocori High School in Cold Spring, Minnesota. The shooter targeted one individual but shot at multiple individuals. While he was shooting in the gym, the coach confronted and stopped the shooter before law enforcement was on scene. Two people were shot; one was killed. (Sources: agency report, SHRs, news articles)

August 27, 2003

A 36-year-old male armed with a 9mm pistol attacked the Windy City Core Supply Inc. located in Chicago, Illinois. The shooter had previously been terminated. Police were on scene 4 minutes after initial notification. The shooter immediately opened fire at police, who backed off. When negotiations did not work, a SWAT team entered the scene approximately 2 hours later and engaged the shooter. After exchanging gunfire, the shooter was fatally wounded. Six people were shot and killed. (Sources: agency report, SHRs, news articles)

July 17, 2003

A 58-year-old male armed with an AK-47 attacked the Kanawha County Board of Education meeting located in Charleston, West Virginia. The shooter entered the meeting through the rear entrance and entered the building through the boiler room. After he attempted to light one board member on fire, three administrators wrestled his weapon away after he got one shot off. The administrators subdued the shooter until police arrived on scene 2 minutes later. One person was shot and survived. (Sources: news articles)

July 8, 2003

A 48-year-old male armed with multiple weapons (.223 semi-automatic rifle and 12-gauge shotgun) attacked the Lockheed Martin factory located in Meridian, Mississippi. The shooter left a mandatory ethics and diversity meeting and returned fully armed. He opened fire on the meeting and then moved to the factory floor. He continued shooting for approximately 7 minutes before killing himself. Police arrived on scene 8 minutes after the initial report and found the shooter dead. Seventeen people were shot, six of whom were killed. (Sources: agency report, SHRs, news articles)

July 2, 2003

A 25-year-old male armed with an unknown-caliber pistol attacked the Modine Manufacturing Co located in Jefferson City, Missouri. The shooter walked throughout the building indiscriminately shooting. He then fled the premises and was confronted by a police officer 8 minutes later. The two exchanged gunfire and the shooter killed himself. Eight people were shot; three were killed. (Sources: SHRs and news articles)

May 9, 2003

A 62-year-old male armed with a semiautomatic rifle attacked Case Western Reserve University located in Cleveland, Ohio. The shooter opened fire throughout the university building. Police were on scene in 4 minutes and exchanged gunfire with the shooter off and on for 7 hours. SWAT team members apprehended the shooter after wounding him in a gun battle. Several people were trapped in their offices throughout the event. Three people were shot; one was killed. (Sources: agency report, SHRs, news articles)

April 24, 2003

A 14-year-old male armed with three pistols (.44–, .357, and .22– caliber) attacked Red Lion Area Junior High located in Red Lion, Pennsylvania. The shooter opened fire in the cafeteria before classes began. He killed himself before police arrived on scene 4 minutes later. One person was shot and died at the scene. (Sources: agency report and news articles)

October 28, 2002

A 41-year-old male armed with five pistols of unknown calibers attacked the University of Arizona College of Nursing located in Tucson, Arizona. The shooter entered the school with a hit list and methodically targeted these individuals and then ordered all of the students out of the building. Police were on scene in 3 minutes and entered the event 6 minutes later; however, the shooter had already killed himself. Three people were shot and killed. (Sources: SHRs and news articles)

October 27, 2002

An 18-year-old male armed with a shotgun attacked multiple locations around Sallisaw, Oklahoma. The shooter was confronted for reckless driving, at which time he began randomly shooting bystanders. He drove along US 64, randomly shooting at cars. After an hour and a half, the shooter ran into a police roadblock where he was taken into custody. Nine people were shot, two of whom were killed. (Sources: SHRs and news articles)

March 22, 2002

A 54-year-old male armed with a .22-caliber rifle and a 12-gauge shotgun attacked Bertrand Products located in South Bend, Indiana. The shooter opened fire at the factory and then fled as law enforcement arrived 2 minutes later. While fleeing, he exchanged gunfire with police and eventually killed himself. Five people were shot, three of whom were killed. (Sources: agency report, SHRs, news articles)

January 16, 2002

A 42-year-old male armed with a .380 pistol attacked the Appalachian School of Law located in Grundy, Virginia. The shooter began the shooting spree in the dean's office and systematically worked his way through the school grounds. Three students—two of whom were off-duty police officers—tackled the shooter as he exited the building. The event was over 5 minutes after it started and before police officers arrived on scene. Six people were shot, three of whom were killed. (Sources: SHRs and news articles)

December 6, 2001

A 36-year-old male armed with a shotgun attacked Nu-Wood Decorative Millwork located in Goshen, Indiana. The shooter had been terminated from employment in the morning; in the afternoon he returned and opened fire during the afternoon shift change. Police were on scene 3 minutes after being initially notified; however, the shooter had already killed himself. The officers were unaware of the situation inside and waited for a SWAT team to arrive. The SWAT team made entry 56 minutes later. Six people were shot; one was killed. (Sources: agency report, SHR, news articles)

April 25, 2001

A 36-year-old female armed with an unknown weapon attacked the Laidlaw Transit Services maintenance yard located in San Jose, California. The shooter walked calmly into the maintenance yard at the start of the morning work shift and opened fire. A co-worker physically subdued her after she fired on co-workers for 3 minutes. Four people were shot; one was killed. (Sources: SHRs and news articles)

March 22, 2001

An 18-year-old male armed with both a 12-gauge shotgun and a .22-caliber pistol attacked Granite Hills High School located in El Cajon, California. The shooter opened fire indiscriminately throughout the school. The timeline is unclear; however, it is known that a police officer shot the shooter to stop the event. Five people were shot; none were killed. (Sources: news articles)

March 5, 2001

A 15-year-old shooter armed with a .22-caliber revolver attacked Santana High School located in Santee, California. The shooter opened fire in the restroom of the school and even reloaded his revolver. An off-duty police officer, at the school registering his child, responded to the sound of gunshots. Fifteen people were shot, two of whom were killed. (Sources: news articles)

January 10, 2001

A 54-year-old male armed with a pistol attacked the Amko Trading store located in Houston, Texas. The shooter was in a personal feud with the business owners. He walked through the front door and opened fire. Police arrived on scene shortly after the incident started. Upon police arrival, the shooter killed himself. Three were shot and killed. (Sources: new articles)

December 26, 2000

A 42-year-old male armed with a semiautomatic rifle and shotgun attacked Edgewater Technology Inc. located in Wakefield,

Massachusetts. The shooter was upset over having his wages garnished to pay back taxes. He targeted individuals related to the accounting department while passing up other potential victims. When police arrived, an unknown amount of time later, they found the shooter sitting down in a conference room. He was apprehended without further incident. Seven people were shot and killed. (Sources: SHRs and news articles)

Index